HEAL

DESSERT COOKBOOK

SUGAR-FREE AND GLUTEN-FREE HEALTHY RECIPES DESSERT COOKBOOK

DIANA POLSKA

CONTENTS

INTRODUCTION

You can eat dessert and still be lean and healthy. Using natural sweeteners instead of sugar to sweeten desserts is a simple way to reduce weight gain caused by the excessive consumption of sweets.

If every bakery, cake maker, chocolate maker and candy manufacturer used stevia or other low glycemic index natural sweeteners instead of sugar, then obesity would not be such a widespread problem in today's society. Dieting or dietary restrictions would not be necessary, and you could eat dessert with every meal if you really wanted to.

HEALTHY INGREDIENTS

For cookies, cupcakes, donuts, muffins, pancakes, waffles, brownies, cakes, pies, and all other desserts and baked goods, you can substitute a few ingredients to make these desserts healthier and lower in calorie density. The two main ingredients to eliminate are white flour and white sugar, as both have high glycemic values, causing blood sugar control problems and weight gain.

You can replace wheat flour with coconut flour, quinoa flour, oat flour, spelt flour, kamut flour, rye flour, barley flour, or buckwheat flour. Coconut flour is a popular choice. It is high in fiber, low on the GI, and gluten-free. Oat flour is another popular choice. It tastes a lot like white flour but is much healthier. It's lower on the GI and is a rich source of soluble fiber.

You can replace white sugar with low GI, natural sweeteners such as pure stevia, coconut palm sugar, sugarcane juice, Manuka honey, and sweet proteins (Brazzein, Thaumatin, Monelin, Curculin, Mabinlin, Miraculin, Pentadin). Not everyone reacts to these sugars the same way, even if they are low in the GI, so it's best to buy a glucose meter and test your blood sugar before and after eating one of these sweeteners to see which works best for you.

UNHEALTHY SWEETENERS

There are many disadvantages of eating sugar. High sugar intake increases advanced glycation end products (AGEs), which are sugar molecules that attach to and damage proteins in the body. AGEs speed up the aging of cells, which may contribute to a variety of chronic and fatal diseases.

Sugar produces a rise in triglycerides, a leading cause of heart disease. Sugar feeds cancer cells and has been connected to the development of cancer of the breast, ovaries, prostate, rectum, pancreas, biliary tract, lung, gallbladder, and stomach. Sugar can also cause arthritis, multiple sclerosis, diabetes, osteoporosis, Alzheimer's disease, cataracts, kidney damage, and adrenal gland dysfunction.

Agave syrup has become popular in recent years but is not a good choice. The Medical Advisory Board of the Glycemic Research Institute (GRI) made the decision to halt all future clinical trials involving Agave as a result of the latest round of GRI Human In Vivo Clinical Trials, in which the diabetic subjects experienced severe and dangerous side effects related to the oral ingestion of the sweetener Agave. The institute also legally de-listed and placed a ban on agave for use in foods, beverages, chocolate and other products.

Artificial sweeteners are not recommended. They have been linked to an increased risk of getting cancer. Long-term use of artificial sweeteners has been linked to headaches, seizures, blindness, and cognitive and behavioral changes.

Artificial sweeteners such as saccharin (Sugar Twin, Sweet 'N Low), aspartame (Equal, NutraSweet), sucralose (Splenda), acesulfame potassium (also known as acesulfame k—Sunett, Sweet One), neotame, and tagatose are linked to a number of health problems. Numerous studies show that frequent consumption of low-calorie artificial sweeteners causes weight gain and increases one's risk for metabolic syndrome, Type 2 diabetes, and cardiovascular disease.

The consumption of artificial sweeteners leads to increased body weight and obesity because it interferes with the normal functions of the body. In several studies, consumption of artificial sweeteners increased BMI and increased body fat percentage at a two-year follow-up.

Even though low-calorie artificial sweeteners are currently approved for use, many people have reported that they believe their negative health symptoms were caused by these artificial sugar substitutes.

HEALTHY SWEETENERS

Coconut palm sugar, stevia, and raw organic Manuka honey are the best natural sweeteners to use and they even have some health benefits.

Coconut palm sugar is a good sugar substitute. It is low on the GI (with a GI of 35), and rich in potassium, magnesium, zinc, iron and B vitamins.

stevia has been widely used for centuries in South America and in Japan. It has zero calories and has a GI of zero, which means it does not raise blood sugar levels. Unlike sugar, which has a negative effect on people with diabetes, stevia has been shown to have a positive effect on those with diabetes. Studies have found that stevia improves insulin sensitivity, promotes additional insulin production, and helps reverse diabetes and metabolic syndrome.

The medicinal use of products made by honeybees is called apitherapy. The use of honey and propolis in the treatment and prevention of numerous diseases has been documented. Honey has demonstrated bactericidal activity against salmonella, Shigella, Escherichia coli, and H. pylori.

Research demonstrates that propolis has the highest antioxidant power, followed by royal jelly and honey. Propolis has antibacterial, antifungal, antiviral, antioxidative, antiparasitic, immunomodulating, anti-inflammatory, analgesic, hepatoprotective and anti-carcinogenic effects. Royal jelly has antitumor effects.

The antibacterial activity in Manuka honey is much stronger than in other types of honey. "UMF" stands for "Unique Manuka Factor" and is a property that gives Manuka honey its special healing quality. UMF Manuka honey with a rating of 16+ has the highest level of antibacterial activity. Manuka honey is best consumed raw, as heat destroys the nutrients in honey.

Lo han guo is an exotic fruit extract that has zero calories and zero glycemic impact, making it safe for diabetics and hypoglycemics to use. Lo han guo can be used in your baking as a sugar substitute.

Xylitol is just as sweet as table sugar (sucrose) but has about 40% fewer calories and 75% fewer carbohydrates. Xylitol also won't raise your blood sugar like regular sugar does, as the body does not require insulin to metabolize xylitol.

Raw honey is a good sugar substitute, has a low glycemic response, and is suitable for those with diabetes. Raw, unprocessed honey has antioxidants, minerals, vitamins, amino acids, enzymes, and phytonutrients. It is considered a "superfood," which is a nutrient-rich food considered to be especially beneficial for health and well-being. It is good for sweetening tea, coffee or drinks. Pasteurized honey has a high GI, so always use raw, unheated honey.

Coconut palm sugar has a lower GI (35) than white sugar does. It is rich in magnesium, potassium, zinc and B vitamins. In terms of taste, out of all the natural sweeteners, it comes closest to white sugar. It's good for baking and sweetening coffee, tea or smoothies.

Raw sugarcane juice has a low GI. It has no simple sugars and doesn't cause blood sugar to soar like white sugar does. It contains calcium, magnesium, potassium, iron, and manganese.

Lucuma powder is made from whole Peruvian lucuma fruit. It is rich in minerals such as iron, zinc, potassium, calcium, magnesium, vitamin B3 and beta carotene. Lucuma has a low GI and GL.

stevia comes in powdered or liquid form. It's a good substitute for white sugar when baking. stevia is sweeter than sugar, so you don't need to use much. It doesn't affect blood sugar levels. It has a GI of zero and has zero calories.

Sweet proteins (Brazzein, Thaumatin, Monelin, Curculin, Mabinlin, Miraculin, Pentadin) have been isolated from plants that grow in tropical rainforests. Sweet proteins are thousands of times sweeter than sucrose. They are of low-calorie value and can safely be used as sweeteners by people suffering from diseases linked to the consumption of sugar e.g. obesity, diabetes, and hyperlipemia.

RECIPES

NUTTY PEACH AND PEAR BARS

Makes:
8-10 Servings

Preparation time:
20 minutes

Ingredients:
2 ripe fresh pears (pitted and sliced) - save one for garnish
3 ripe fresh peaches (cored and sliced) - save one sliced peach for garnish
¼ cup pistachios
¼ cup walnuts
2 Tbsp. lime juice
3 eggs
1 cup coconut cream
¼ cup coconut sugar
½ tsp. salt
½ tsp. vanilla extract
Coconut oil (to grease pan)

Directions:

1. Grease a square baking dish with coconut oil.
2. In the food processor, place 2 peaches (chunks), 1 of the pear chunks, the lime juice, and 3 Tbsp. of coconut sugar.
3. Once it has become a puree, set it aside.
4. In a mixing bowl, combine the eggs, salt and the rest of the coconut sugar. Whisk well.

5. In a saucepan, boil some water and place the bowl with the egg mixture over the boiling water for just 3 or 4 minutes. This should allow the mixture to become your filling (the texture is similar to a pudding). Set aside and let it cool off for 10 minutes.

6. Mix together the fruit mixture and vanilla extract.

7. Add the egg mixture to the puree. Finally, add the walnuts and pistachios to the mixture.

8. Pour the fruity mixture into the dish, cover it with plastic wrap, then refrigerate for at least 12 hours; overnight works well.

9. When serving, use freshly sliced peach and pear to decorate, and you could also sprinkle with coconut sugar.

10. Cut the bars to the size you like and enjoy them with a nice cup of tea.

Nutrition Information per serving: 169 Calories, 7 g total fat, 60 mg cholesterol, 36 mg sodium, **22 g carbonates (sugars),** 2.1g fiber, and 4g protein.

HEALTHY FRUIT POPSICLES

Makes:
16-24 Servings

Preparation time:
5 minutes

Ingredients:
1 large jar unsweetened applesauce (your favorite brand)
1 Tsp. lemon juice
1 pinch ground cinnamon
1 cup fresh blueberries
1 cup fresh blackberries

Directions:

1. Wash the berries and set them aside.

2. In a large bowl, combine the applesauce, lemon juice, cinnamon, and fruits. Pour the mixture into Popsicle molds.

3. You could also use some ice trays and put Popsicle sticks in them (cut in halves if needed).

4. Place in the freezer for at least 12 hours (overnight).

5. Lick away!

Nutrition Information per serving: 39 Calories, 7.5 g total fat, 0 mg cholesterol, 1 mg sodium, **8.5 g carbonates (sugars),** 1g fiber, and 0.5g protein.

CUTE FRUIT BITES

Makes:

12-14 Servings

Preparation time:

30 minutes

Ingredients:

2 cups pineapple juice
1 cup orange juice
1 cup mango juice
3 envelopes unflavored gelatin (dry)
1 cup small pineapple chunks

Directions:

1. In a bowl, toss the gelatin powder over the orange, mango and pineapple juices.

2. If needed, add a little hot water to help the gelatin dissolve.

3. Pour this mixture into a square baking dish.

4. Place the dish in the freezer for about 40 minutes.

5. When you remove it, add the pineapple chunks.

6. Keep this mixture in the refrigerator until you're ready to serve it. Cut in small or big squares (kids and adults will love these!).

Nutrition Information per serving: 130 Calories, 0.2 g total fat, 0 mg cholesterol, 31 mg sodium, **22.2 g carbonates (sugars),** 1.2.g fiber, and 2g protein.

ALMOND BUTTER SNACKS

Makes:
18-20 Servings

Preparation time:
15 minutes

Ingredients:
1/3 cup almond butter
¼ cup coconut oil
1 cup raw Manuka honey
1 cup coconut flour
¼ cup unsweetened coconut flakes
¼ cup flaxseeds
¼ cup chopped almonds
½ tsp. ground nutmeg

Directions:

1. In a medium size pot, mix the almond butter, coconut oil, and honey. Bring to boil.

2. Remove the mixture from the heat; add the rest of the ingredients.

3. Transfer the mixture into a mixing bowl and let it cool off for 5 minutes.

4. Use your hands to prepare the balls.

5. Adjust coconut flour or coconut oil if you are not satisfied with the texture.

6. Refrigerate the small almond snacks in a plastic container.

Nutrition Information per serving: 103 Calories, 5.5 g total fat, 1.2 mg cholesterol, 68 mg sodium, **11.1 g carbonates (sugars),** 2.1g fiber, and 2g protein.

PEACH MELBA

Makes:
6 Servings

Prep:
10 minutes

Ingredients:
1 Tbsp. raspberry naturally flavored tea mix (make sure it's low calories and sugar-free)
1 Tbsp. peach naturally flavored tea mix (make sure it's low calories and sugar-free)
1 cup cold water
1 small package sugar-free raspberry flavored gelatin
1 small package sugar-free raspberry flavored gelatin
2 cups boiling water
1 cup sliced peaches (frozen or canned are okay; just make sure they are sugar-free)
Coconut cream if desired

Directions:

1. In a medium size bowl, dissolve both tea mixes with some cold water.

2. Dissolve the gelatin in a different mixing bowl by pouring hot water on it.

3. Add the tea mixture to the gelatin mixture and refrigerate the combination.

4. After about an hour, you should be left with a mixture that is somewhat firm.

5. Using your favorite serving cups, pour 1 cup of the gelatin mix, add some peaches and some coconut cream (to taste).

6. Refrigerate the mixture until you're ready to serve it (it should be cooled down for at least 4-5 hours before being eaten).

Nutrition Information per serving: 35 Calories, 5.5 g total fat, 1.2 mg cholesterol, 38 mg sodium, **5.1 g carbonates (sugars),** 1.9g fiber, and 1g protein.

SUGARLESS PEACH COBBLER

Makes:
6 Servings

Preparation time:
35 minutes

Ingredients:

Filling

1 large can no sugar added peaches (save the juice)
2 Tsp. raw organic Manuka honey
1 Pinch ground cinnamon
2 Tbsp. coconut oil (room temperature)

Crust (topping)

5 Tbsp. oat flour
1/4 cup coconut oil (room temperature)
4 Tbsp. coconut palm sugar
1 Pinch salt
Some water

Directions:

1. Preheat oven to 325 degrees F.

2. Prepare a large baking dish by greasing it with a little coconut oil.

3. For the filling, simply mix all the ingredients together, except the peaches.

4. Place the peaches on the bottom of the dish and pour the mixture on top.

5. For the topping, mix the ingredients in a separate bowl first and add some water to it to get the desired consistency.

6. Finally, sprinkle the crust on top of the peaches.

7. Bake in the oven for about 30 minutes.

Nutrition Information per serving: 290 Calories, 24.5 g total fat, 0 mg cholesterol, 108 mg sodium, **21.5 g carbonates (sugars),** 13g fiber, and 1.5g protein.

NUTRITIVE COOKIES

Makes:
16-20 Servings

Preparation time:
15 minutes

Ingredients:
2 Tbsp. finely chopped walnuts
1 Tbsp. finely chopped sunflower seeds
½ cup chopped dried dates
1 Tbsp. pure stevia
1 cup almond flour
½ tsp. baking soda
2 Tbsp. coconut oil (room temperature)
4 Tbsp. unsweetened apple juice

Directions:

1. Preheat oven to 325 degrees F.

2. In a food processor, place the walnuts, sunflowers, and dates, then turn it on a few times. The blend will be a little pasty.

3. Place the mixture of nuts and dates in a large mixing bowl. Add the almond flour, baking soda, and stevia to it. Stir well.

4. Add to the mixture the coconut oil and apple juice. Stir it again. Your cookie dough should be ready to bake.
5. On a greased baking sheet, drop the cookie dough (about a teaspoon each), while making sure there is at least an inch between each drop.

6. Bake the dough in the oven for about 10 minutes.

7. Let the cookies cool down before you store them a container.

Nutrition Information per serving: 69 Calories, 3 g total fat, 0 mg cholesterol, 41 mg sodium, **9 g carbonates (sugars),** 1 g fiber, and 1g protein.

ANYTIME ENERGY BARS

Makes:
24 Servings

Preparation time:
45 minutes

Ingredients:
2 cups quinoa flour
¼ cup flaxseeds
1/2 tsp. baking soda
1 pinch salt
1 tsp. ground cinnamon
3/4 cup natural (unsweetened) smooth peanut butter
½ cup Manuka honey
2 large eggs
2 Tbsp. walnut oil
3/4 cup dried cherries
3/4 cup chopped almonds

Directions:

1. Preheat oven to 350 degrees F.

2. Grease a rectangle baking dish with a little coconut oil or non-stick cooking spray.

3. In a large mixing bowl, combine the first 5 ingredients.

4. In a different bowl, mix the peanut butter, eggs, and honey.

5. Combine the 2 mixtures together and stir well.

6. Finally, add the dried cherries and almonds. Mix again.

7. Pour the mixture into the baking dish. Bake in the oven for about 25 minutes.

8. Let it cool off before you start cutting.

Nutrition Information per serving: 172 Calories, 7.9 g total fat, 10 mg cholesterol, 68 mg sodium, **23 g carbonates (sugars),** 2g fiber, and 4g protein.

BANANA FUN TREATS

Makes:

4 Servings

Preparation time:

5 minutes

Ingredients:

2 Tbsp. shredded coconut

2 Tbsp. Low-fat no sugar added yogurt

2 Tbsp. almond butter

2 bananas

Directions:

1. Choose to roast the shredded coconut or not. If you choose to, the easiest way to do this is to heat the shredded coconut for a few minutes in coconut oil, in a skillet.

2. Slice the bananas in half.

3. In a bowl, mix the yogurt and almond butter. Spread the mixture on each banana half and sprinkle some shredded coconut on top of them.

Nutrition Information per serving: 69 Calories, 2 g total fat, 60 mg cholesterol, 32 mg sodium, **11 g carbonates (sugars),** 1.1g fiber, and 3g protein.

STRAWBERRY MOUSSE

Makes:
8-10 Servings

Preparation time:
20 minutes

Ingredients:

1 X 8 ounces package low fat cream cheese (room temperature)
1 cup unsweetened coconut milk (divided)
3 Tbsp. strawberry natural flavoring (natural drink mix, exclude any drink mix with artificial sweeteners)

Directions:

1. Beat the cream cheese in a medium mixing bowl and start adding to it half of the required strawberry flavoring mix. (I highly suggest using an electric mixer, so it is easier to get to the wanted consistency).

2. Alternate adding the coconut milk and the rest of the strawberry mix to the first mixture. Continue mixing.

3. Refrigerate the mousse for about 3 hours before serving. (I like to serve this dessert in fancy cups!).

Nutrition Information per serving: 85 Calories, 3 g total fat, 3 mg cholesterol, 130 mg sodium, **9 g carbonates (sugars),** 0g fiber, and 5g protein.

PERFECTLY ACCEPTABLE BROWNIES

Makes:
12-16 Servings

Preparation time:
1 hour

Ingredients:
1 cup unsalted grass fed butter
2 Tbsp. unsweetened cashew milk
1 ½ coconut palm sugar
5 large eggs
1 tsp. pure vanilla
8 Tbsp. unsweetened cocoa powder

Directions

1. Preheat oven to 350 degrees F.

2. In a small saucepan, heat on low the butter, the cashew milk and the cocoa powder. Whisk so no lumps form.

3. In a bowl, mix together the eggs and coconut palm sugar.

4. Slowly pour the chocolate mixture, and stir constantly.

5. In a greased square pan, pour the mixture and bake it for about 45 to 50 minutes.

6. These brownies will be fluffy. Let them cool down before you start cutting them into squares.

Nutrition Information per serving: 55 Calories, 50 g total fat, 44 mg cholesterol, 10 mg sodium, **3 g carbonates (sugars),** 1g fiber, and 7g protein.

LEMON DELIGHT

Makes:
10-12 Servings

Preparation time:
35 minutes

Ingredients:
Crust
1 cup quinoa flour
1 pinch salt
2 Tbsp. coconut palm sugar
1 Tbsp. coconut oil (room temperature)
2 Tbsp. grass fed butter
1 Tbsp. sugar cane juice
Filling
1/4 cup coconut flour (fine ground)
½ cup. Coconut palm sugar
2 Tbsp. Manuka honey
5 medium eggs
1/2 cup lemon juice

Directions

1. Preheat oven to 350 degrees F. With some coconut oil, lightly grease a square or rectangle baking dish.

2. Prepare the crust by combining the quinoa flour, salt, and coconut palm sugar.

3. In a different bowl, mix the coconut oil, butter and sugar cane juice. Mix well. The mixture might still be crumbly and that is okay.

4. Press the crust into the baking dish and bake for about 15 minutes.

5. Meanwhile, prepare the filling by combining all the listed ingredients and using the electric mixer to get a smooth consistency.

6. When you remove the crust from the oven, pour the lemon mixture on it and then put it back in the oven for another 15 minutes or so.

7. When done, let it cool down completely before cutting and serving it.

Nutrition Information per serving: 90 Calories, 6 g total fat, 57 mg cholesterol, 52 mg sodium, **3 g carbonates (sugars),** 0.8g fiber, and 3.1g protein.

YOU NEW FAVORITE CHOCOLATE COOKIES

Makes:

24 Servings

Preparation time:

45 minutes

Ingredients:

½ cup unsweetened cocoa powder

1 pinch of salt

½ cup stevia (divided)

1 tsp. pure almond extract

1 Tbsp. almond flour

1 Tbsp. coconut palm sugar

1/8 tsp. cream of tartar

3 medium size eggs

Directions:

1. Preheat oven to 325 degrees F.
2. In a bowl, combine the cocoa powder, ¼ cup stevia, and salt.
3. In a different mixing bowl, use the electric mixer to beat the eggs and the cream of tartar, as well as the rest of the stevia.
4. Combine the two mixtures and stir.
5. Use a teaspoon to drop the chocolate dough on a greased baking sheet.
6. Bake the dough in the oven for about 30 minutes.

Nutrition Information per serving: 25 Calories, 0.9 g total fat, 3 mg cholesterol, 13 mg sodium, **6 g carbonates (sugars),** 1g fiber, and 1.2g protein.

DARKER ANGEL FOOD CAKE

Makes:
10-12 Servings

Preparation time:
1.5 hours

Ingredients:
1 cup almond flour
½ cup quinoa flour
1 cup powdered sweet proteins such as Monelin, Curculin
⅓ cup unsweetened cocoa powder
½ tsp. ground nutmeg
9 egg whites (room temperature)
1 tsp. cream of tartar
1Tbsp. pure almond extract

Directions:

1. Preheat oven to 375 degrees F.

2. In a large bowl, mix the dry ingredients; Almond flour, quinoa flour, ½ of the suggested amount of sweet proteins sugar, cocoa powder, and nutmeg.

3. With a good whisk or an electric mixer, bring the egg whites to foam. Add the cream of tartar to it, as well as the rest of the sugar and almond extract. You should continue mixing until the mixture forms some peeks.

4. Add the dry ingredients to the egg mixture and mix it well. Pour the mixture into a greased baking cake dish of your choice. Ideally, an angel cake food pan.

5. Bake for about 50 minutes. Check with a knife to make sure it comes back out clean, and then you know it's done.

Nutrition Information per serving: 125 Calories, 1 g total fat, 15 mg cholesterol, 47 mg sodium, **26 g carbonates (sugars),** 1g fiber, and 5g protein.

PEACH AND STRAWBERRY SHAKE

Makes:
2 Servings

Preparation time:
5 minutes

Ingredients:
2 fresh peaches (peeled, pitted and sliced)
½ cup fresh strawberries (sliced)
2 cups skim milk
1 pinch ground ginger

Directions:

1. Place the washed and sliced peaches and strawberries in your high-speed blender.

2. Add the milk and the ginger. Activate the blender until the texture is smooth.

3. Serve in 2 tall glasses, or save one in the fridge for later that day.

Nutrition Information per serving: 101 Calories, 0.1 g total fat, 15 mg cholesterol, 65 mg sodium, **22 g carbonates (sugars),** 3g fiber, and 5g protein.

CHOCOLATE AND COFFEE MERINGUES

Makes:
36 Servings

Preparation time:
1 hour 20 minutes

Ingredients:
2 Tbsp. unsweetened cocoa powder
1 Tbsp. almond flour
½ tsp. instant coffee powder
Whites of 3 medium size eggs
½ cup pure stevia

Directions:

1. Preheat oven to only 250 degrees F.

2. In a bowl, mix together the cocoa powder, almond flour, and coffee powder.
3. Whisk the egg whites with the sugar (add gradually) until it gets foamy (I suggest you use the electric mixer; it will be much easier).

4. Add the cocoa mixture to this last mix.

5. Drop a spoonful of mixture on the greased baking sheet and bake the meringues for about an hour.

6. When the time's up, let them cool off so they can get crunchy.

Nutrition Information per serving: 12 Calories, 0 g total fat, 0 mg cholesterol, 11 mg sodium, **3.2 g carbonates (sugars),** 0g fiber, and 0g protein.

BREAKFAST OR DESSERT SMOOTHIE

Makes:

2 Servings

Preparation time:

10 minutes

Ingredients:

2 Tbsp. coconut flour
2 Tbsp. flax seeds
2 frozen bananas
3 cups unsweetened coconut milk
1 Tbsp. sugarcane juice
1 pinch ground cinnamon

Directions:

1. Of course, you can always slightly modify the ingredients. For example, if you are not a big fan of coconut milk, use almond or cashew milk; just make sure you use the unsweetened kind.

2. Place all the ingredients listed above in the blender.

3. Activate the blender on high speed until the mixture is completely smooth and drinkable through a straw.

4. Pour the drink in your favorite cups or glasses.

5. Cheers!

Nutrition Information per serving: 179 Calories, 1 g total fat, 101 mg cholesterol, 39 mg sodium, **17 g carbonates (sugars),** 3.1g fiber, and 1g protein.

GREEN BUT SWEET SMOOTHIE

Makes:

2 Servings

Preparation time:

12 minutes

Ingredients:

2 cups unsweetened cashew milk

1 cup chopped fresh spinach

1 Tbsp. flaxseeds

¼ cup ice cubes

2 Tbsp. Manuka honey

Directions:

1. Add all the ingredients in the blender, and blend until the mixture is smooth.
2. This drink is low in carbs, but certainly loaded with antioxidants—drink up!

Nutrition Information per serving: 115 Calories, 1.3 g total fat, 15 mg cholesterol, 150 mg sodium, **24 g carbonates (sugars),** 2g fiber, and 3g protein.

CHEESE AND PEARS DELICIOUS COMBO

Makes:
4 Servings

Preparation time:
1.5 hour

Ingredients:
2 ripe and sliced pears, (cored also)
1 Tbsp. fresh lemon juice
1/4 cup low fat shredded sharp Cheddar cheese
½ cup coconut flour
1 Tbsp. pure stevia
½ tsp. ground cinnamon
2 Tbsp. coconut oil (melted)

Directions:

1. Preheat oven to 425 degrees F.

2. Place the sliced pears on the bottom of a greased baking dish and drizzle the lemon juice on them.

3. Sprinkle the shredded cheese on top of the pears.

4. In a small bowl, prepare the crust by mixing the coconut flour, stevia, cinnamon and coconut oil.

5. Sprinkle the coconut flour mixture on top of the dish and bake in the oven for about 20 minutes.

6. Remove the food from the oven when the cheese is completely melted.

Nutrition Information per serving: 202 Calories, 5 g total fat, 25 mg cholesterol, 160 mg sodium, **23 g carbonates (sugars),** 3.9g fiber, and 7g protein.

ZUCCHINI CHOCOLATE BREAD

Makes:
16 Servings

Preparation time:
1.5 hour

Ingredients:
1 cup shredded zucchinis (1 medium)
⅔ Cup Manuka honey
⅔ cup unsweetened cocoa powder
½ cup apple juice
2 medium size eggs
2 cup almond flour
1 tsp.; baking powder
1 tsp. baking soda
1 tsp. ginger
1 tsp. all spices
1 pinch salt

Directions:

1. Preheat oven to 350 degrees F.

2. In a mixing bowl, combine the dry ingredients including the almond flour, baking powder, soda, salt, ginger and all spices.

3. In a medium size saucepan, place the apple juice, cocoa powder, and honey. Put the heat on low until all is mixed well and set aside.

4. Add the eggs into the cooled down chocolate mixture.

5. Put the almond flour mixture into the chocolate one and stir the mix until no lumps are seen.

6. Finally, add the shredded zucchinis and mix again.

7. Pour the chocolate batter into a greased cake or bread pan.

8. Bake for about 55 minutes to an hour.

9. Let it cool down before slicing and tasting.

Nutrition Information per serving: 115 Calories, 1.3 g total fat, 15 mg cholesterol, 150 mg sodium, **24 g carbonates (sugars),** 2g fiber, and 3g protein.

BANANA FRENCH TOASTS EGG-FREE

Makes:
2 Servings

Preparation time:
15 minutes

Ingredients:
1 ripe banana
1 tablespoon fresh lime or lemon juice
¼ teaspoon ground nutmeg
2 slices of diabetic friendly bread (light Tapioca or almond flour bread)
Coconut oil

Directions:

1. In a small bowl, whisk the ripe banana and the lemon juice with nutmeg (you are basically making the equivalent of French toasts but without eggs).

2. Heat the coconut oil over medium heat in a skillet.

3. Dip the slices of bread in your banana mix.

4. Cook the bread on each side until they're golden.

5. You can cut the bread in quarters for finger bites.

Nutrition Information per serving: 132 Calories, 2 g total fat, 0 mg cholesterol, 149 mg sodium, **27 g carbonates (sugars),** 4g fiber, and 4g protein.

CHOCOLATE AND CHERRIES LOW CARBS CAKE

Makes:
10- 12 Servings

Preparation time:
1.5 hour

Ingredients:
2 cups quinoa flour
1 cup pure stevia
½ cup unsweetened cocoa powder
2 Tbsp. coconut oil
2 large eggs
1 tsp. pure vanilla
1 tsp. baking powder
½ tsp. baking soda
1 pinch salt
1 1/2 cup fresh cherries (pitted)
½ cup sugar-free cherry jam
Some water

Directions:

1. Preheat oven to 350 degrees F.
2. Mix the following together in a large mixing bowl: flour, stevia, cocoa powder, salt, baking soda and baking powder.
3. In another bowl, combine the yogurt, coconut oil and vanilla.

4. Whisk the eggs and add them to the yogurt mixture. Stir well.

5. Gradually incorporate the wet mixture into the dry one until the batter is ready and there are no lumps.

6. Pour the batter into a square greased baking dish and bake it for about 40 minutes.

7. Meanwhile, in a small saucepan, heat up the cherries, cherry jam, and water. Mix together well.

8. Once the cake is done, let it cool down.

9. When serving, pour some of the cherry mixture on top.

Nutrition Information per serving: 201 Calories, 3.3 g total fat, 111 mg cholesterol, 178 mg sodium, **40 g carbonates (sugars),** 3g fiber, and 5g protein.

THE PERFECT LOW SUGAR FLAN

Makes:
6 Servings

Preparation time:
2 hours

Ingredients:
4 cups skim milk
¼ c unsweetened cocoa powder
1/2 tsp. ground cinnamon
½ tsp. nutmeg
1 cup coconut palm sugar
1 tsp. almond extract
4 large eggs
3 Tbsp. tab water

Directions:

1. Preheat oven to 350 degrees F.

2. In a large pot, combine the skim milk, cocoa powder, cinnamon, nutmeg and ½ cup coconut palm sugar, while setting the temperature on medium heat.

3. Continue cooking for about 20 minutes, and stir frequently. Set aside.

4. In a different saucepan, mix the remaining coconut palm sugar with water. Bring it to boil so it dissolves completely and gets thicker. Cook the syrup until it darkens so it can be your top coat.

5. Grease a large round baking dish that is oven safe.

6. The final step is to whisk the eggs, add the milk, and the almond extract. Then pour the mixture into the greased dish.

7. Add the syrup that you created on top of the mixture and bake it for about 40 minutes. The flan should be firm when you get it out of the oven.

8. Let it cool down before serving or cutting.

Nutrition Information per serving: 250 Calories, 5.3 g total fat, 150 mg cholesterol, 119 mg sodium, **34 g carbonates (sugars),** 1g fiber, and 10g protein.

NO FLOUR VANILLA AND ALMOND CAKE

Makes:
10-12 Servings

Preparation time:
1 hour

Ingredients:
3 Tbsp. unsweetened vanilla proteins powder
1 cup raw sliced almonds
1 cup coconut palm sugar (divided)
½ cup low-fat sour cream
1 Tbsp. coconut oil
2 large egg yolks
1 Tbsp. almond extract
5 large egg whites (room temperature)
1 pinch salt

Directions:

1. Preheat oven to 350 degrees F. Also, prepare a cake baking pan with either coconut oil or cooking spray.

2. In the food processor, grind the almonds until they become powdery.

3. Mix the protein powder with a little water and then add to it the grounded almonds, sour cream, egg yolks, coconut oil, ½ cup coconut palm sugar and almond extract.

4. Combine the egg whites and salt using an electric mixer, until peaks form.

5. Transfer the egg whites to the protein powder mixture, and fold.

6. Pour the new mixture into the can pan and bake it for about 35 minutes.

7. Once done, let the cake cool down. You can also sprinkle some coconut palm sugar on top.

Nutrition Information per serving: 175 Calories, 3.3 g total fat, 20 mg cholesterol, 84 mg sodium, **21 g carbonates (sugars),** 2g fiber, and 4g protein.

CHOCOLATE COOKIES WITH PEPPERMINT SPLASH

Makes:

36 Servings

Preparation time:

1 hour

Ingredients:

1/2 cup grass fed butter (room temperature)
3/4 cup pure stevia
1 large egg
1 tsp. almond extract
1/3 cup unsweetened cocoa
2 cups quinoa flour
1 tsp. Baking powder
1 tsp. baking soda
1 pinch salt
½ crushed peppermint candies (sugar-free kind)

Directions:

1. Preheat oven to 350 degrees F.

2. Using an electric mixer, mix the butter, adding the sugar, and mix until it's creamy.

3. Add the egg and almond extract next. Mix well.

4. Add also the quinoa flour, baking soda, baking powder and salt to the original mixture.

5. Add the crushed peppermint candy into the batter.

6. Drop one tablespoon at a time (or if you want to make them smaller, a teaspoon at a time) on a previously greased cookie sheet.

7. Bake the cookies in the oven for about 12 minutes.

Nutrition Information per serving: 75 Calories, 2.7 g total fat, 20 mg cholesterol, 90 mg sodium, **12 g carbonates (sugars),** 0.2g fiber, and 1.2g protein.

A SIMPLY DELICIOUS PINEAPPLE CAKE

Makes:

12 Servings

Preparation time:

1 hour

Ingredients:

1 can unsweetened pineapple slices (keep the juice also)
2 Tbsp. Manuka honey
1 tsp. cinnamon
1 cup coconut palm sugar
¼ cup coconut oil (room temperature)
2 egg whites
1/2 teaspoon pure vanilla
1 ½ cup almond flour
1/2 teaspoon baking soda

Directions:

1. Preheat oven to 375 degrees F.

2. Grease a cake pan with some coconut oil. Set it aside.

3. Separate the pineapple slices from its juice. Place the pineapple slices at the bottom of the pan. You guessed it; it will be an upside down cake!

4. Drizzle the honey on the fruits and also sprinkle evenly the cinnamon. Set it aside.

5. In a large mixing bowl, combine the egg whites, vanilla, coconut palm sugar and coconut oil. Add the dry ingredients next: almond flour, baking soda and also the pineapple juice. Mix well. You may use your electric mixer.

6. Once well mixed, pour the batter on top of the pineapple slices and bake them in the oven for about 30 minutes.

7. You will enjoy this delicious fruity cake.

Nutrition Information per serving: 165 Calories, 4 g total fat, 0 mg cholesterol, 108 mg sodium, **27 g carbonates (sugars),** 2g fiber, and 1g protein.

A CHOCOLATE BREAD DELIGHT IDEA

Makes:
8 Servings

Preparation time:
1 hour

Ingredients:
1/4 cup pure stevia
2 Tbsp. unsweetened cocoa powder
1 1/2 cups unsweetened almond milk
3 large
1 tsp. lemon zest
1 tsp. pure almond extract
1 tsp. ground cinnamon
4 cubes whole grains bread or sourdough bread
Optional: store bought 1 chocolate syrup

Directions:

1. Preheat oven to 350 degrees F.

2. In a large bowl, combine the stevia and cocoa. Add to it the almond milk, eggs, almond extract, cinnamon and lemon zest.

3. In a greased large baking pan (coconut oil works), place all the bread cubes.

4. Add the mixture to the baking pan and bake for about 40 minutes.

5. Serve the chocolate bread warm and drizzle it with some sugar-free chocolate syrup if you choose to.

Nutrition Information per serving: 130 Calories, 2 g total fat, 130 mg cholesterol, 80 mg sodium, **23 g carbonates (sugars),** 1g fiber, and 6g protein.

CRANBERRY PINEAPPLE BREAD PUDDING

Makes:
9 Servings

Preparation time:
50 minutes

Ingredients:
2 cups cinnamon swirl or sugar-free chocolate swirl bread (cubes)
1/4 cup dried cranberries
2 cups unsweetened coconut milk
2 scoops sugar-free vanilla proteins powder
2 eggs
1 can pineapples sugar-free (cubes)
1 tsp. ground cinnamon

Directions:

1. Preheat oven to 350 degrees F.

2. You can choose to prepare this dish in individual oven safe cups or in a large dish. Let's choose a large baking pan for this example.

3. Grease the rectangle baking dish with coconut oil and place the bread cubes evenly on the bottom of it.

4. On top of the bread, pour the pineapple cubes and cranberries.

5. In a large mixing bowl, combine the rest of the ingredients and stir. Then pour the custard on top.

6. Bake the pudding for 35 minutes, and serve it warm with fresh cream if you'd like to.

Nutrition Information per serving: 75 Calories, 1 g total fat, 2 mg cholesterol, 180 mg sodium, **11 g carbonates (sugars),** 1g fiber, and 4g protein.

THE PERFECT CAKE DUO: CHOCOLATE AND PUMPKIN

Makes:

24 Servings

Preparation time:

1 hour

Ingredients:

1 cup tapioca flour
1 cup coconut flour
3/4 cup coconut palm sugar
1 tsp. baking powder
1 tsp. baking soda
2 tsp. all spices
1 can sugar-free pumpkin puree
3 medium size eggs
¼ coconut oil (room temperature)
3 Tbsp. sugarcane syrup
1 ½ cup fat-free cream cheese (room temperature)
2 additional Tbsp. coconut palm sugar
¼ cup unsweetened chocolate chips

Directions:

1. Preheat oven to 325 degrees F.

2. Use a mixing bowl to combine the dry ingredients: flour, coconut palm sugar, baking soda, baking powder, and spices.

3. In a different bowl, mix the wet ingredients: pumpkin puree, eggs, coconut oil and sugarcane syrup.

4. Combine both mixtures and stir until the texture is super smooth.

5. Pour the batter into a large square dish and bake it for about 30 minutes.

6. Time to make the cheese frosting. In a bowl, use the electric mixer to bring to a fluffy texture the cream cheese and 2 tbsp. Coconut palm sugar.

7. When the cake is done, frost it with the cream cheese frosting and sprinkle some chocolate chips on top.

Nutrition Information per serving: 170 Calories, 4 g total fat, 20 mg cholesterol, 170 mg sodium, **15 g carbonates (sugars),** 2g fiber, and 3g protein.

MANGO CREPES

Makes:
4 Servings

Preparation time:
1 hour

Ingredients:
1 ripe mango (peeled, pitted, cubed)
¼ cup dried golden raisins
2 tsp. lemon juice
½ tsp. nutmeg
½ tsp. cinnamon
2 Tbsp. walnut oil
1/4 cup low sugar mango or orange juice
1 Tbsp. pure stevia
3/4 teaspoon cornstarch
½ tsp. vanilla extract
4 prepared crêpes (almond or coconut flour)

Directions:

1. In a large saucepan, cook on medium/low heat the mango, walnut oil, dried raisins with lemon juice and spices, for about 30 minutes.

2. Meanwhile, prepare your favorite crepes recipe.

3. Also, in a small saucepan, prepare the syrup for the mango crepes: mix the mango juice with the stevia, cornstarch, and vanilla.

4. Start setting up the crepes; one per person, with a generous filling of mango mixture. Fold each crepe and drizzle a tablespoon of the syrup on top.

5. Enjoy for dessert or for a delicious breakfast.

Nutrition Information per serving: 240 Calories, 9 g total fat, 100 mg cholesterol, 221 mg sodium, **32 g carbonates (sugars),** 3g fiber, and 6g protein.

SUGARCANE FLAVORED CUSTARD

Makes:

6 Servings

Preparation time:

1 hour

Ingredients:

2 cups heavy cream

2 eggs

¼ cup coconut palm sugar

2 Tbsp. sugarcane syrup

3 cups boiling water

1 pinch cinnamon

Directions:

1. Preheat oven to 300 degrees F.

2. Prepare 6 small oven-safe ramequins with non-stick cooking spray.

3. In a bowl, mix the heavy cream, eggs, coconut palm sugar and cinnamon.

4. Pour the mixture equally into each ramequin.

5. Pour the boiling water into a large rectangle dish and place the ramequins inside it. Bake for a little over an hour.

6. Combine half-and-half, egg substitute, sugar, vanilla, and nutmeg in a large bowl. Pour this mix into the prepared custard cups.

7. Serve with some sugarcane syrup on top, if you wish.

Nutrition Information per serving: 130 Calories, 1 g total fat, 20 mg cholesterol, 139 mg sodium, **23 g carbonates (sugars),** 0g fiber, and 5.1g protein.

CHOCOLATE CREPES WITH FRUITS

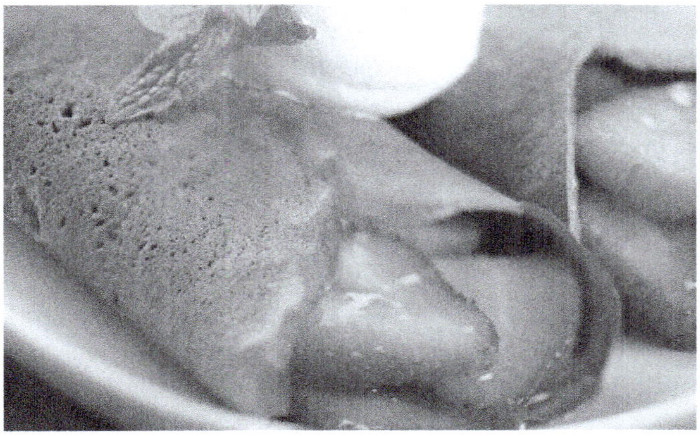

Makes:
8 Servings

Preparation time:
1 hour

Ingredients:
1 cup quinoa flour
1 cup cashew milk
2 Tbsp. unsweetened cocoa powder
3 egg whites
2 Tbsp. pure stevia
2 Tbsp. coconut oil
3 cups of your favorite berries: blueberries, strawberries, raspberries, blackberries ...
2 Tbsp. Manuka honey
1 pinch salt

Directions:

1. Let's prepare the chocolate crepes first.

2. Combine the quinoa flour, egg whites, stevia, coconut oil and cocoa powder. Stir for a while until the mixture is smooth.

3. Heat coconut oil in a small skillet and pour enough for a crepe at a time. Cook as many crepes as you need.

4. Meanwhile, in a small saucepan, place the berries chosen with a few tablespoons of water and 2 Tbsp. of Manuka honey. Bring the mixture to a boil and then set it aside to cool.

5. Fill each chocolate crepe with the berry mixture. Serve warm.

Nutrition Information per serving: 280 Calories, 8 g total fat, 56 mg cholesterol, 387 mg sodium, **52 g carbonates (sugars),** 5g fiber, and 9g protein.

DELECTABLE PEANUT COOKIES

Makes:
24 Servings

Preparation time:
1 hour

Ingredients:
¼ cup coconut or walnut oil
¾ natural no sugar added peanut butter
¼ cup unsweetened apple juice
1 cup quinoa flour
1 Tbsp. flaxseeds
1 egg
1 tsp. almond extract
1 tsp. baking soda
1 pinch salt
¼ cup raw peanuts (optional)

Directions:

1. Preheat oven to 350 degrees F.

2. In a large mixing bowl, mix the butter and peanut butter well. Then add the egg, apple juice, and almond extract.

3. Finally add the rest of the ingredients: flour, flaxseeds, baking soda, and salt. If you choose to add peanuts, it's time to add them as well.

4. Mix well and then on a greased cookie sheet, place teaspoons full of dough. You should have enough batter for about 24 cookies, so you might need 2 baking sheets.

5. Bake the cookies for 10 minutes. Enjoy them with a glass of skim milk.

Nutrition Information per serving: 100 Calories, 3 g total fat, 10 mg cholesterol, 88 mg sodium, **9 g carbonates (sugars),** 1g fiber, and 3g protein.

SWEET TEA FOR DESSERT

Makes:

4 Servings

Preparation time:

50 minutes

Ingredients:

1 pinch ground cinnamon
1 pinch ground ginger
3 cups water
4 green or black tea bags (your favorite)
2 cups unsweetened coconut milk
3 Tbsp. pure sugarcane syrup

Directions:

1. Boil the 3 cups of water in a medium size pot and add the tea and the spices. Let it simmer for 12-15 minutes.

2. Remove the tea bags and then add coconut milk and sugarcane syrup.

3. Stir the sweet tea well and keep it warm until you serve it (if you wish to serve it warm).

4. If you would like to transform this drink into a frozen one, cover the liquid and freeze it for about 1 hour and then use a fork to break the frozen drink into crystals (it's refreshing during the summer season!).

Nutrition Information per serving: 93 Calories, 0.2 g total fat, 2 mg cholesterol, 58 mg sodium, **20 g carbonates (sugars),** 0g fiber, and 4g protein.

CUPCAKES FROM THE ISLANDS

Makes:

24 Servings

Preparation time:

1 hour

Ingredients:

1 package sugar-free white cake mix
1 can unsweetened crushed pineapple with their juice
2 egg whites
1 Tbsp. coconut oil (room temperature)
½ cup shredded unsweetened coconut
1 Tbsp. orange zest
1 Tbsp. lemon juice
1 Tbsp. chia seeds

Directions:

1. Preheat oven to 350 degrees or to whatever temperature the cake mix package says.

2. Grease 24 muffin tins ahead and set them aside.

3. In a large bowl, combine the cake mix, egg whites, coconut oil, lemon juice and orange zest. You can use a wooden spoon or the electric mixer if you prefer.

4. Pour the batter into the muffin tins evenly. Sprinkle with chia seeds before placing it in the oven.

5. Bake the batter for about 15-20 minutes.

6. Meanwhile, prepare the topping by mixing in a skillet on medium heat the crushed pineapples, juice and shredded coconut. Cook the mixture for 10 minutes or until you are happy with the color of the coconut. It will caramelize and will make the perfect topping once your cupcakes have cooled down. Yummy!

Nutrition Information per serving: 144 Calories, 2 g total fat, 9 mg cholesterol, 155 mg sodium, **24 g carbonates (sugars),** 1g fiber, and 5g protein.

SUPER CLASSIC BREAD PUDDING

Makes:
8-12 Servings

Preparation time:
55 minutes

Ingredients:
2 cups unsweetened almond milk
4 egg whites
3 Tbsp. coconut palm sugar
2 Tbsp. melted coconut oil
1 tsp. almond extract
12 slices of whole wheat bread with cinnamon swirl cut into cubes
3/4 cup dried cherries

Directions:

1. Preheat oven to 350 degrees F.

2. Prepare a square baking dish by greasing it with coconut oil.

3. In a large bowl, mix the egg whites, coconut palm sugar, almond extract and almond milk.

4. When the mixture is smooth, add the bread cubes and then the dried cherries. Let it soak for about 10 minutes.

5. Pour everything into the greased dish and bake the pudding in the oven for 40 minutes.

Nutrition Information per serving: 150 Calories, 2 g total fat, 2 mg cholesterol, 214 mg sodium, **26 g carbonates (sugars),** 1g fiber, and 6g protein.

SOUR CREAM AND NUT CAKE

Makes:
12-16 Servings

Preparation time:
1.5 hour

Ingredients:
1/2 cup unsweetened pear and applesauce
½ cup coconut oil (room temperature)
3/4 cup pure stevia
2 large eggs
1 cup fat-free sour cream
1 Tbsp. Manuka honey
1 1/2 cups almond flour
1 1/2 cups coconut flour
1 tsp. baking powder
½ tsp. baking soda
1 pinch salt
2 Tbsp. coconut palm sugar
1 tsp. ground cinnamon
1/2 cup chopped almonds

Directions:

1. Preheat oven to 350 degrees F.

2. Mix together first the coconut oil, pear and applesauce, and stevia in a large bowl.

3. Add to the dry mixture the eggs, sour cream and honey. Use the electric mixer to facilitate mixing until it is smooth.

4. Add the coconut and almond flours, baking soda, baking powder, and salt.

5. Prepare the middle section by mixing in a separate bowl the almonds, cinnamon and some the coconut palm sugar.

6. Pour half of the batter into a greased square pan and then sprinkle it with the nut mixture.

7. Pour the other half of the batter and bake it for about 50 minutes or until done.

Nutrition Information per serving: 180 Calories, 4 g total fat, 35 mg cholesterol, 200 mg sodium, **26 g carbonates (sugars),** 2g fiber, and 4g protein.

CHERRY DELIGHT

Makes:
10 Servings

Preparation time:
45 minutes

Ingredients:
2 Tbsp. non-salted butter
1/2 cup fresh pitted cherries
1 cup coconut palm sugar
1/4 cup chopped walnuts
1 cup quinoa flour
1 tsp. baking powder
½ tsp. salt
1 tsp. allspices
2 large eggs
1 cup unsweetened soy milk
1 Tbsp. pure sugar cane syrup
¼ cup coconut oil (room temperature)

Directions:

1. Heat oven to 350 degrees F.

2. Pour the melted butter into a round baking pan.

3. In a bowl, mix the cherries, half of the coconut palm sugar and the walnuts.

4. Sprinkle the cherry mixture onto the coconut oil on top of the butter evenly.

5. Mix the remaining ingredients in a large bowl to create the cake batter.

6. Pour the batter on top of the cherries without mixing them.

7. Bake it for about 35 minutes. Let the cake cool down for 10 minutes before turning it upside down ... Voila!

Nutrition Information per serving: 165 Calories, 4 g total fat, 2 mg cholesterol, 289 mg sodium, **17 g carbonates (sugars),** 4g fiber, and 4g protein.

PEANUT BUTTER BROWNIES

Makes:
12 Servings

Preparation time:
45 minutes

Ingredients:
¼ non-salted butter
½ cup unsweetened cocoa powder
1/3 cup sugar-free peanut butter
¾ cup coconut palm sugar
¼ cup water
1/4 cup butter
2 large eggs
¼ sesame oil
1 ½ cup cashew flour (almond flour might be easier to find)
3/4 cup refrigerated or frozen egg product, thawed, or 3 eggs, lightly beaten
¼ cup unsweetened pieces of dark chocolate

Directions:

1. Preheat oven to 375 degrees F.

2. In a saucepan, combine the butter, coconut palm sugar and water over low heat. Remove the mix from the heat and add the eggs and sesame oil. Mix well.

3. Add half of the required flour to the first mixture and mix it well. Set it aside.

4. In a different bowl, mix the peanut butter with half of the created batter.

5. In a second bowl, do the same but with the cocoa powder.

6. Combine both batters to create swirls.

7. In a square greased pan, alternate dropping the peanut butter and chocolate batter, and create the wanted designs.

Nutrition Information per serving: 152 Calories, 8.5 g total fat, 6 mg cholesterol, 61 mg sodium, **17.5 g carbonates (sugars),** 1g fiber, and 3.5g protein.

THE ALMOST TOO GOOD TO BE TRUE DESSERT

Makes:

4 Servings

Preparation time:

25 minutes

Ingredients:

4 peeled tangerines or 8 clementines (depending on the season and what's available)
3 Tbsp. coconut palm sugar
1 tsp. ground clove
1 Tbsp. arrowroot starch
½ cup water
1 cup coconut flour
3 Tbsp. shredded coconut
1 pinch nutmeg
Sugar-free whipped topping (optional)

Directions:

1. Preheat oven to 425 degrees F.

2. Prepare the syrup by mixing in a saucepan the arrowroot starch, coconut palm sugar, and spices. Gradually add the water and stir the mix until it thickens.

3. Stir in the citrus fruits (in portions of course).

4. Prepare the topping by mixing the flour, nutmeg, and shredded coconut. Set it aside.

5. Place the fruit in the bottom of a greased dish and sprinkle the topping on them.

6. Bake the fruit for about 30 minutes. When it comes out of the oven, serve it with sugar-free whipped topping.

Nutrition Information per serving: 170 Calories, 3.5 g total fat, 7 mg cholesterol, 111 mg sodium, **34 g carbonates (sugars),** 3g fiber, and 4g protein.

DELICIOUS SQUARE BERRIES

Makes:
12 Servings

Preparation time:
45 minutes

Ingredients:
Filling:
1/3 cup pure stevia
1 envelope unflavored gelatin
1 pound fresh raspberries
1 cup fresh blackberries

Crust
1 cup coconut flour
2 Tbsp. melted non-salted butter
2 Tbsp. Manuka honey
Topping: sugar-free whipped cream if you like

Directions:

1. Preheat oven to 400 degrees F.

2. To make the crust, mix the ingredients in a bowl and then place at the bottom of a square greased baking pan. Bake them for about 20 minutes. Set them aside.

3. Meanwhile, let's make the filling.

4. Combine in a saucepan the berries, sugar, and gelatin. Cook the mix on medium heat and stir it until it's dissolved properly. You will need to let it cool off before using it.

5. Once the crust and the filling are cooled enough, pour the filling on top of the crust. Refrigerate the dessert for at least a few hours. Lastly, cut it into squares and serve it with some whipped cream.

Nutrition Information per serving: 139 Calories, 4 g total fat, 7 mg cholesterol, 80 mg sodium, **25 g carbonates (sugars),** 1g fiber, and 2g protein.

HERBS AND MELON FROZEN TREATS

Makes:

8 Servings

Preparation time:

20 minutes + hours in freezer

Ingredients:

1/4 cup coconut palm sugar

¼ cup water

2 tbsp. Fresh chopped mint

1 Tbsp. lime juice

1 tsp. lime zest

1 medium honeydew melon (peeled, seeded and cubed)

Directions:

1. In a saucepan, we will prepare the syrup by combining the sugar and the water.

2. Bring the liquid to boil and stir it until it's all dissolved. Add the mint. Set it aside.

3. Mix the melon in a high-speed blender until it is a smooth texture.

4. Add to it the mint syrup you created, and blend again.

5. Place the mixture in a freezer-friendly container and cover it with foil.

6. After 2 or 3 hours, you should be able to use a fork to scrape the mixture into crystals and serve this frozen treat in a fancy bowl or cup. Enjoy!

Nutrition Information per serving: 45 Calories, 2g total fat, 20 mg cholesterol, 10 mg sodium, **11g carbonates (sugars),** 1g fiber, and 1g protein.

STRAWBERRY AND CHEESE LOG

Makes:
10-12

Preparation time:
2 hours

Ingredients:
Cake
3 eggs (room temperature when ready to use)
¾ cup almond flour
1 tsp. baking powder
1 pinch salt
1 pinch cinnamon
¾ cup pure stevia
1 Tbsp. orange juice
2 ripe bananas
Filling
1/3 cup sugar-free whipped cream
1 package fat-free cream cheese
1 cup chopped fresh strawberries

Directions:

1. Preheat your oven to 375 degrees F. Grease a rectangle baking pan with coconut oil or non-stick cooking spray. Set aside.

2. In a bowl, combine the flour, baking powder, cinnamon, and salt.

3. In a different bowl, beat the eggs, I highly suggest you use an electric mixer for this one. Add gradually the stevia, bananas, and orange juice. Pour the flour into the egg mixture. Mix it well. You now have your cake batter.

4. Spread the batter evenly in a greased baking pan. Bake it for 15-18 minutes.

5. When the cake comes out of the oven, transfer it to a dish and roll it into a log.

6. Prepare the filling by mixing all ingredients.

7. After about 45 minutes, remove the towel from the cake and unroll it. Spread evenly the berry filling, and roll the cake again.

8. Cut the cake into slices and enjoy a beautiful and delicious log cake filled with goodness.

Nutrition Information per serving: 168 Calories, 3.5 g total fat, 69 mg cholesterol, 164 mg sodium, **28 g carbonates (sugars),** 1g fiber, and 4g protein.

SIMPLE BANANA BREAD

Makes:

8-10 Servings

Preparation time:

1 hour

Directions:

1 1/3 cups quinoa flour
½ cup pure stevia
1 tsp. tsp. baking powder
½ baking soda
1 pinch salt
1 Tbsp. walnut oil
1/3 cup coconut cream
2 or 3 ripe bananas
1 tsp. almond extract
1/3 cup chopped pecans

Directions:

1. Preheat oven to 350 degrees F.

2. Combine all the dry ingredients: quinoa flour, baking soda, baking powder, salt, and stevia.

3. Add the walnut oil, coconut cream and the bananas (mashed).

4. Add the pecans; stir some more. Then pour the batter into a loaf pan to bake.

5. Bake bread for about 50 minutes or until done.

Nutrition Information per serving: 160 Calories, 4.5 g total fat, 0 mg cholesterol, 170 mg sodium, **89.5 g carbonates (sugars),** 2g fiber, and 4g protein.

EVERYDAY MUFFINS

Makes:

12 Servings

Preparation time:

45 minutes

Ingredients:

1/4 cup unsweetened applesauce
1 large egg
2 cups unsweetened coconut milk
2 Tbsp. vanilla protein powder
3 tablespoons coconut oil (room temperature)
1 pinch salt
3/4 cup coconut palm sugar
1 ½ cup coconut flour
½ cup flaxseeds
1 Tbsp. baking soda
1 tsp. cinnamon
Optional: Dried fruits (raisins, cranberries or cherries if you want)

Directions:

1. Preheat oven to 350 degrees F.

2. Prepare 12 muffin tins by greasing them with coconut oil.

3. Combine together the egg, applesauce, coconut milk, protein powder, coconut oil, salt and coconut palm sugar in a large bowl. Mix well.

4. Add the rest of the ingredients and mix again until you obtain a muffin batter. If you choose to add dried fruits, add them at the end before mixing again.

5. Fill the muffin cups 2/3 and bake the muffins for about 25 minutes.

Nutrition Information per serving: 150 Calories, 7.5 g total fat, 20 mg cholesterol, 230 mg sodium, **22 g carbonates (sugars),** 3g fiber, and 5g protein.

SPICY CARROT BITES

Makes:
12-16 Servings

Preparation time:
50 minutes

Ingredients:
¾ cup almond flour
½ cup pure stevia or equivalent
1 1/2 teaspoons pumpkin pie spice
½ tsp. ground ginger
½ tsp. ground nutmeg
¾ cup finely shredded carrots
¾ cups chopped pecans or almonds
2 large eggs
¼ cup unsweetened almond milk
¼ cup coconut oil (room temperature)
Frosting (optional) use sugar-free of course

Directions:

1. Preheat oven to 350 degrees F.

2. First of all, in a large bowl, combine the first 5 dry ingredients. Mix well.

3. Add the carrots, nuts, eggs, coconut oil and almond milk. Stir well. Your mixture should be ready.

4. Grease a square baking dish and pour the batter on it.
5. Bake the batter in the oven for about 20 minutes.
6. Frost the bites with your store-bought or homemade sugar-free favorite frosting, if you wish.

Nutrition Information per serving: 121 Calories, 7 g total fat, 5 mg cholesterol, 61 mg sodium, **12 g carbonates (sugars),** 1g fiber, and 2.5g protein.

DRESSED UP PEACHES

Makes:
6 Servings

Preparation time:
5 minutes

Ingredients:
¼ cup goat cheese (room temperature)
1 Tbsp. Manuka honey
1 pinch nutmeg
2 Tbsp. chopped walnuts
4-6 peaches (pitted and cut in halves)
½ cup Fresh berries (blueberries, raspberries or other)
Fresh chopped mint to garnish

Directions:

1. In a bowl, prepare the cheese filling by mixing the goat cheese, honey, nuts, and nutmeg. Set the mix aside in the refrigerator.

2. Place one half peach in a bowl and about one large tablespoon of fresh berries, topped with the cheese filling. Decorate it with mint.

Nutrition Information per serving: 144 Calories, 6 g total fat, 0 mg cholesterol, 11 mg sodium, **21 g carbonates (sugars),** 1g fiber, and 4g protein.

CARROT MUFFINS FOR EVERYONE

Makes:
12 Servings

Preparation time:
45 minutes

Ingredients:
1 1/3 cup quinoa flour
2 Tbsp. chai seeds
1 tsp. baking powder
1/2 tsp. baking soda
1/2 tsp. ground cinnamon
1 pinch salt
1 large egg
2 large eggs
6 Tbsp. dried sweet proteins (such as Brazzein, Curculin, Mabinlin or Pentadin)
1/2 cup unsweetened pear and applesauce
1/4 cup coconut oil
2 tsp. lemon zest
1 Tbsp. sugarcane juice
1 1/2 cups shredded carrots
1/2 cup golden dried raisins

Directions:

1. Preheat oven to 350 degrees F.

2. Combine in a large bowl the quinoa flour, chia seeds, baking powder, baking soda, salt and cinnamon.

3. In a different bowl, mix the eggs and sweet proteins. Add the apple and pear sauce, coconut oil, lemon zest and sugarcane juice. Mix it well and also add the golden raisins and carrots.

4. Add the dry mixture to the wet one and mix them together thoroughly.

5. Fill 12 previously greased muffin cups.

6. Bake the muffins for about 25-30 minutes or so.

Nutrition Information per serving: 180 Calories, 6 g total fat, 20 mg cholesterol, 10 mg sodium,25 **g carbonates (sugars),** 2g fiber, and 3g protein.

UNIQUE RASPBERRY SOUP

Makes:
4-6 Servings

Preparation time:
35 minutes

Ingredients:
1 ½ cup fresh raspberries
1 cup cranberry juice
¼ cup coconut palm sugar
1 Tbsp. orange juice
1 cup low fat sour cream
1/3 cup coconut cream
1 tsp. cinnamon
1 cup water

Directions:

1. Mix the raspberries with water in a high-speed blender.

2. Pour the mixture into a saucepan and add to it the cranberry, orange juices, coconut palm sugar, and cinnamon.

3. Bring the mixture to a boil and then turn the heat down on low for it to simmer.

4. Add the coconut milk and keep it warm until it's time to serve.

5. When serving, drop a tablespoon of sour cream in each bowl. Decorate the soup with raspberries, if you like.

Nutrition Information per serving: 240 Calories, 3 g total fat, 15 mg cholesterol, 50 mg sodium, **43 g carbonates (sugars),** 5g fiber, and 5g protein.

WHO WANTS SUSHI?

Makes:
12 Servings

Preparation time:
50 minutes

Ingredients:
2 bananas
¼ cup almond butter
1 Tbsp. coconut flour
¼ cup unsweetened coconut flakes

Directions:

1. Peel your bananas. Spread almond butter all over each banana (a nice rich coat).
2. Slice each banana into 6 thick portions.
3. Roll each "sushi piece" into the mixture of flour and coconut flakes.
4. Pack the food in your kid's lunchbox, or serve it any day of the week.

Nutrition Information per serving: 102 Calories, 1 g total fat, 12 mg cholesterol, 60 mg sod um, **15 g carbonates (sugars),** 1g fiber, and 1.2g protein.

RASPBERRY AND POPPY SEED MUFFINS

Makes:
12 Servings

Preparation time:
40 minutes

Ingredients:
1 cup fresh washed raspberries
¼ cup coconut oil
¼ cup reduced fat goat cheese
½ cup coconut palm sugar
1 egg
2 cups coconut flour
1 cup skim milk
2 Tbsp. poppy seeds

Directions:

1. Preheat oven to 400 degrees F.

2. Grease 12 muffin tins or plate the paper liners in each of them (your choice).

3. Make sure after washing the raspberries that you drain them well.

4. Mix together the goat cheese (that is room temperature) with the coconut oil) so that it is soft. You can use an electric mixer to make sure the combination gets smoother.

5. Add the egg and milk and then gradually the coconut flour and coconut palm sugar as well. Continue mixing.

6. Add the raspberries and poppy seeds. Mix gently and pour the batter into each muffin tin.

7. Bake it for a little less than 30 minutes.

Nutrition Information per serving: 150 Calories, 6 g total fat, 20 mg cholesterol, 240 mg sodium, **5.5 g carbonates (sugars),** 1g fiber, and 4g protein.

DELICIOUS DIP FOR YOUR FAVORITE FRUITS

Makes:
8 Servings

Preparation time:
10 minutes

Ingredients:
2 cups fat-free sour cream
2 Tbsp. Manuka honey
1 Tbsp. orange zest
2 Tbsp. no sugar added orange juice
Fresh fruits to serve with (strawberries, cherries or other)

Directions:

1. Mix the orange juice, orange zest, sour cream and honey together, then refrigerate the mix. Serve in a tightly closed container.

2. Prepare the fresh fruits by washing them and cutting them to the size you want. This dip could easily be served with pieces of mellow such as honeydew or cantaloupe.

Nutrition Information per serving: 48 Calories, 1.2 g total fat, 63mg cholesterol, 41 mg sodium, **10 g carbonates (sugars),** 1g fiber, and 1g protein.

SWEET POTATOES CASSEROLE

Makes:
8 Servings

Preparation time:
1 hour

Ingredients:
4 large peeled sweet potatoes
¼ cup coconut cream
2 eggs
1 tsp. vanilla extract
½ tsp. cinnamon
½ tsp. nutmeg
½ cup coconut palm sugar
¼ cup coconut oil (room temperature)
¼ cup sugarcane juice
¼ chopped walnuts
1/3 cup coconut flour
3 Tbsp. quinoa flour
1 pinch salt

Directions:

1. Preheat oven to 375 degrees F.

2. Prepare a large baking dish by greasing it with coconut oil.

3. Boil some water in large saucepan and after dicing the sweet potatoes, cook them for 20 minutes or until tender.

4. Mash the potatoes once they're cooked and then add the coconut oil, salt, eggs, vanilla, cinnamon, nutmeg and coconut palm sugar.

5. Transfer the mixture to the baking dish.

6. In a separate mixing bowl, mix the sugarcane juice, salt, quinoa flour and coconut flour. Sprinkle the sweet potatoes with the flour mixture.

7. Bake the food for about 30 minutes and then serve it warm.

Nutrition Information per serving: 230 Calories, 7 g total fat, 65 mg cholesterol, 150 mg sodium, **36g carbonates (sugars),** 2g fiber, and 5g protein.

DRIED CRANBERRY AND WALNUT SCONES

Makes:
12 Servings

Preparation time:
45 minutes

Ingredients:
2 eggs
1/3 cup walnut oil
1 cup pure stevia
3/4 cup skim milk
½ tsp. vanilla extract
2 cups quinoa flour
1 cup fresh cranberries
¼ cup chopped walnuts
½ tsp. baking soda
½ tsp. baking powder
2 Tbsp. Manuka honey

Directions:

1. Spray the muffin tins with non-stick baking oil. Set it aside.

2. Preheat oven to 375 degrees F.

3. Whisk the eggs, walnut oil vanilla and milk together in a large mixing bowl.

4. In a different bowl mix the dry ingredients: baking powder, baking soda and quinoa flour.

5. Combine both mixtures together next and also add the cranberries, nuts, and honey. Mix again well.

6. Pour the batter into the muffin tins (it should fill about 10-12 spaces). Bake it for about 20 minutes or so.

Nutrition Information per serving: 210 Calories, 7 g total fat, 20 mg cholesterol, 130 mg sodium, **33 g carbonates (sugars),** 1g fiber, and 5g protein.

BANANA AND ALMOND BUTTER SMOOTHIE

Makes:
4 Servings

Preparation time:
5-8 minutes

Ingredients:
1 small sliced ripe banana
1/2 cup nonfat sour cream
3 Tbsp. almond butter
3 Tbsp. Manuka honey
1 large ripe and sliced banana
Some ice

Directions:

1. Simply blend all the ingredients in your high-speed blender. Add as much ice as you like.

2. Pour your smoothie into a tall glass. Enjoy!

Nutrition Information per serving: 120 Calories, 4 g total fat, 0 mg cholesterol, 100 mg sodium, **16 g carbonates (sugars),** 1g fiber, and 6g protein.

CRISPY TREAT

Makes:
6 Servings

Preparation time:
20 minutes

Ingredients:
6 slices bread (made with quinoa flour)
2 cups unsweetened shredded coconut
2 cups coconut flour
1 Tbsp. ground cinnamon
4 large eggs
1 Tsp. almond extract
½ cup coconut palm sugar
1 ½ cup coconut cream
Optional: fruits on the side

Directions:

1. Preheat oven to 375 degrees F.

2. Combine the coconut cream, coconut palm sugar, eggs, and almond extract. Whisk well together.

3. In a bowl, mix the dry ingredients (coconut flour, shredded coconut, cinnamon).

4. Cut the slices into triangles or squares.

5. Dip bread pieces into the coconut cream mixture, and then into the flour mixture.

6. Place the mixture on a greased baking sheet and bake it for about 10 minutes.

7. Serve with a diabetic-friendly dip and fresh fruits.

Nutrition Information per serving: 300 Calories, 9 g total fat, 155 mg cholesterol, 460 mg sodium, **27 g carbonates (sugars),** 3g fiber, and 12g protein.

YOGURT DIP

Makes:
12 Servings

Preparation time:
10 minutes

Ingredients:
½ cup low-fat sugar-free vanilla yogurt
½ cup sugar-free whipped cream
1 Tbsp. sugarcane juice
Serve with fresh fruits instead of crackers if you can

Directions:

1. Put the yogurt, whipped topping, and sugarcane juice in the blender.
2. Blend the mix until it's smooth.
3. Serve the dip with your favorite fruits.

Nutrition Information per serving: 100 Calories, 1.5 g total fat, 5 mg cholesterol, 95 mg sodium, **16 g carbonates (sugars),** 1.g fiber, 3g protein.

THE SMOOTHEST PIE

Makes:
12 Servings

Preparation time:
25 minutes

Ingredients:
2 cups freshly sliced peaches or peaches from a can (make sure then they are sugar-free)
½ cup freshly pitted cherries (cut in halves)
1 cup almond flour
2 Tbsp. pure stevia
1 envelope unflavored gelatin
½ cup skim milk
1 tsp. almond extract
1 cup sugar-free marshmallow cream
¼ cup melted ghee butter
Coconut oil to grease

Directions:

1. Preheat oven to 375 degrees F.
2. Prepare the crust by mixing the almond flour and stevia in a bowl. Add the melted butter and mix well.
3. In a dish greased with coconut oil place the crust at the bottom. Bake it for 10 minutes.
4. Meanwhile, prepare the pie filling by mixing the marshmallow cream, milk and unflavored gelatin.
5. Pour the pie filling into the pie crust (when it's cooled down) and refrigerate it for a few hours.
6. Decorate the pie with peaches and cherries.

Nutrition Information per serving: 170 Calories, 7 g total fat, 18 mg cholesterol, 126 mg sodium, **24 g carbonates (sugars),** 1g fiber, and 3g protein.

DRIED FRUIT AND NUT SQUARES

Makes:
12 Servings

Preparation time:
1.5 hour

Ingredients:
Nonstick cooking spray (coconut oil if you can)
3 Tbsp. gee butter
3-4 cups quinoa flour small pretzels (broken into small pieces)
¾ cups dried pineapple pieces
1 cup sunflower seeds
½ cup coconut flour
2 Tbsp. sugarcane juice
3 Tbsp. Sugar-free caramel sauce
1 pinch salt

Directions:

1. Place parchment paper in a large baking dish.

2. Melt the butter in a saucepan over medium heat, then stir in the sugar cane juice and caramel. Mix well. Wait until the mix becomes thicker before removing it from the heat.

3. Stir in the pretzels pieces, sunflower seeds, dried pineapple, coconut flour, and mix well.

4. The mix will be sticky, but go ahead and press the mixture into the dish that you set aside previously, and refrigerator it for an hour.

5. Remove the food the refrigerator and cut it into squares or rectangles. Place the squares into a hermetically sealed container.

6. Eat only one at a time—if you can!

Nutrition Information per serving: 170 Calories, 8.5 g total fat, 5 mg cholesterol, 183 mg sodium, **29 g carbonates (sugars),** 1g fiber, and 4g protein.

WARM VANILLA BEVERAGE

Makes:
1 serving

Preparation time:
12 minutes

Ingredients:
3/4 cup unsweetened almond milk
2 Tbsp. coconut palm sugar
1/4 tsp. almond extract

Directions:

1. Serving a warm and healthy glad of sweet milk is always welcome, especially on a cold day perhaps.

2. Simply combine all the ingredients in a small saucepan over low heat.

3. Once it's warm enough, transfer it into a cup and enjoy it!

Nutrition Information per serving: 2 Calories, 8.5 g total fat, 6 mg cholesterol, 95 mg sodium, **9 g carbonates (sugars),** 1g fiber, and 6g protein.

MELON SALAD

Makes:
8 Servings

Preparation time:
10 minutes

Ingredients:
1 small cantaloupe (peeled and diced)
1 cup watermelon
1 cup diced pineapple
1 Tbsp. lemon juice
1 Tbsp. lime juice
¼ cup Manuka honey
A few finely chopped mint leaves

Directions:
1. Mix the lime and lemon juice with the honey, in a small bowl.
2. Prepare all the fruits by cutting them in the size you prefer, in a large bowl.
3. Add the citrus juice and honey to the fruit and mint leaves. Stir well.
4. Serve cold.

Nutrition Information per serving: 80 Calories, 0 g total fat, 0 mg cholesterol, 61 mg sodium, **19 g carbonates (sugars),** 1g fiber, and 1g protein.

GINGERBREAD LOAF

Makes:

12-18 Servings

Preparation time:

1 hour

Ingredients:

2 cups unsweetened applesauce
¾ cup sugarcane juice
1/3 cup coconut oil
3 egg whites
1 cup pure stevia
1 cups quinoa flour
1 Tbsp. baking soda
1 tsp. baking powder
1 pinch salt
1 tsp. ginger
1 tsp. nutmeg
1 tsp. cinnamon

Directions:

1. Preheat oven to 350 degrees F.

2. In a large mixing bowl, combine the sugarcane juice, coconut oil, and egg whites. Mix well.

3. In a separate bowl, combine the dry ingredients (baking powder, baking soda, flour and all spices).

4. Combine the wet and dry mixture. Mix well.

5. Add the applesauce to the mixture and stir it.

6. Pour the bread batter into a previously greased baking dish (loaf dish).

7. Bake the bread for about 50 minutes and serve it warm or cold.

Nutrition Information per serving: 180 Calories, 5 g total fat, 35 mg cholesterol, 240 mg sodium, **28.5 g carbonates (sugars),** 1g fiber, and 3g protein.

PEANUT BUTTER COOKIES

Makes:
16 Servings

Preparation time:
15 minutes

Ingredients:
1/2 cup coconut palm sugar
3 Tbsp. Manuka honey
5 Tbsp. coconut oil (room temperature)
¼ cup creamy no sugar added peanut butter
2 eggs
1 tsp. vanilla
1 3/2 cup almond flour
1/2 tsp. baking soda
1 pinch salt

Directions:

1. Preheat oven to 375 degrees F.

2. In a large mixing bowl, combine the honey, coconut oil, eggs, vanilla and peanut butter. Make a smooth mixture.

3. In a separate bowl, mix the flour, baking soda, salt and coconut palm sugar.

4. Combine the dry mixture with the wet and mix them together well.

5. You now have the peanut butter cookies batter ready.

6. Drop about one teaspoon of the batter at a time onto the baking sheet. You should be able to make about 16-20 cookies.

7. Bake the batter for about 10-12 minutes.

8. Enjoy the cookies with a glass of skim milk, or with black coffee.

Nutrition Information per serving: 60 Calories, 20 g total fat, 0 mg cholesterol, 65 mg sodium, **9 g carbonates (sugars),** 0g fiber, and 1g protein.

A LITTLE SOMETHING TO TOP OFF A FRUIT SALAD

Makes:

6 Servings

Preparation time:

20 minutes

Ingredients:

1 cup fresh sliced strawberries
1 cup fresh raspberries
1 cup fresh blueberries
1 cup diced cantaloupe
1 cup diced Granny smith apple (I prefer to leave the peel on)
2 Tbsp. lime juice

Yogurt dip
1 Tbsp. pumpkin pie spice
2 cups low-fat sugar-free plain yogurt
2 Tbsp. Manuka honey

Directions:

1. Prepare all the fresh fruits in a large bowl. Drizzle the lime juice on the fresh fruits to make sure they don't turn brown.

2. Prepare the yogurt dip in a separate bowl by mixing the yogurt, pumpkin spice and honey.

3. Serve anytime of the year; it is always so refreshing and delicious!

Nutrition Information per serving: 170 Calories, 2 g total fat, 5mg cholesterol, 35 mg sodium, **39 g carbonates (sugars),** 1g fiber, and 7g protein.

APPLE AND RAISIN TOPPING

Makes:
6 Servings

Preparation time:
12 minutes

Ingredients:
3 diced red delicious apple or Gala; your choice
2 Tbsp. ghee butter
3 Tbsp. dried raisins
1/2 tsp. ground cinnamon
1/2 Tsp. minced fresh ginger

Directions:

1. After getting all the ingredients ready, warm up the butter in the skillet and sauté the apples with the spices and dried raisins.

2. Remember, this is a topping you can use on applesauce, on your diabetic friendly French toasts or on pancakes. Just delicious!

Nutrition Information per serving: 203 Calories, 2.1 g total fat, 62 mg cholesterol, 189 mg sodium, **41 g carbonates (sugars),** 1.2g fiber, and 6g protein.

FUN POPSICLES

Makes:
10-12 Servings

Preparation time:
15 minutes

Ingredients:
1 package of unsweetened drink mix (lemonade flavor is great)
1 cup pure stevia
2 quarts cold water
12-16 popsicles sticks- molds

Directions:

1. Mix the lemonade mix and the water in a large pitcher. Mix well and add also the stevia. Mix again.
2. Pour the drink mixture into your popsicles molds and freeze them.
3. Lick away!

Nutrition Information per serving: 85 Calories, 0 g total fat, 0 mg cholesterol, 45 mg sodium, **7 g carbonates (sugars),** 0.1g fiber, and 0.5g protein.

VERY BERRY SMOOTHIE

Makes:
2 Servings

Preparation time:
10 minutes

Ingredients:
2 cups unsweetened vanilla cashew milk
1 Tbsp. Manuka honey
1/2 cup fresh raspberries
1/2 cup fresh blueberries
1 Tbsp. lemon juice

Directions:

1. Blend all the ingredients in your high-speed blender until the texture is smooth.

2. Pour the mix into a tall glass. Save a few fresh fruits on the side to decorate your smoothie with.

Nutrition Information per serving: 152 Calories, 8.5 g total fat, 6 mg cholesterol, 61 mg sodium, **17.5 g carbonates (sugars),** 1g fiber, and 3.5g protein.

APPLE CRUMBLE

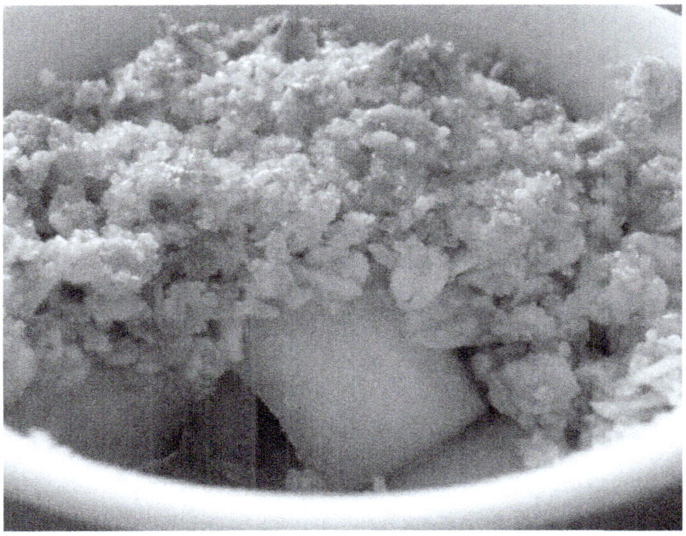

Makes:
6 Servings

Prep:
50 minutes

Ingredients:

1/3 cup coconut flour
3 Tbsp. coconut oil
3 Tbsp. coconut palm sugar
3 Tbsp. water
1 -1.5 pound of your favorite apples: Granny Smith, Gala or Red delicious)

Directions:

1. Preheat oven to 300 degrees F.

2. In a mixing bowl, combine the flour and the room temperature coconut oil; it should be crumbly. Add the coconut palm sugar and mix some more. Set it aside.

3. Slice the apples thinly or into cubes and then place them evenly in a rectangle baking dish.

4. I use also coconut oil to grease the dish. Sprinkle the coconut mixture on top and place the dish in the oven.

5. Bake the apples for about 40 minutes. Serve them warm with sugar whipped cream

Nutrition Information per serving: 320 Calories, 5.2 g total fat, 0 mg cholesterol, 201 mg sodium, **25.2 g carbonates (sugars),** 1.2.g fiber, 7g protein.

DELICIOUS BITES

Makes:
24 Servings

Preparation time:
25 minutes

Ingredients:
2 cups gluten-free and sugar-free cereals (similar to cornflakes)
½ cup almond flour
3/4cup creamy sugar-free peanut butter
1 large egg
1 cup pure stevia
2 tbsp. Vanilla
½ cup golden dried raisins

Directions:

1. Preheat oven to 375 degrees F.

2. In a large bowl, mix the chosen cereals, stevia, almond flour, and raisins.

3. In a different bowl, mix the peanut butter, egg, vanilla, and ginger.

4. Pour the second mixture over the first, and combine gently.

5. After greasing one or two baking sheets, drop about a tablespoon of the mixture at a time.

6. Bake for about 10-12 minutes. Set the bites aside and store them in an airtight container when they've cooled down.

Nutrition Information per serving: 60 Calories, 7 g total fat, 0 mg cholesterol, 42 mg sodium, **8g carbonates (sugars),**1.2g fiber, and 2g protein.

MIXED APPLE SAUCE

Makes:
4 Servings

Preparation time:
35 minutes

Ingredients:
2 ripe Bartlett pears
2 apples (your choice)
2 Tbsp. orange juice
1 Tbsp. lemon juice
2 Tbsp. Manuka honey
½ tsp. nutmeg
½ tsp. cinnamon

Directions:

1. Cut the fruit into small pieces and place all of them in a medium size saucepan.

2. Add the orange juice, lemon juice, honey and spices. Bring to boil. If needed, add a little water. When boiling, reduce the heat to low, and cook for 25 minutes.

3. Place it in the blender and turn it into a puree.

Nutrition Information per serving: 95 Calories, 2 g total fat, 0 mg cholesterol, 1mg sodium, **21 g carbonates (sugars),**2g fiber, and 1g protein.

"BLUE" GRANITA

Makes:
4 Servings

Preparation time:
15 minutes

Ingredients:
1 1/4 cups tab water
2 cups fresh blueberries
¼ cup coconut palm sugar
1 Tbsp. sugar-free cranberry juice
½ Tbsp. minced fresh mint leaves

Directions:

1. Place all ingredients, except the mint leaves, in your high-speed blender. Blend until the mixture is fine.

2. Place the mixture into a baking dish of your choice, knowing it will need to fit in your freezer for an hour or so.

3. Cover the dish with foil and freeze it for about 30 minutes at a time. Remove it from the freezer, then crush the frozen berries with a fork each time before placing the dish back in the freezer.

4. Repeat this step 5 or 6 times.

5. Serve the berries in your favorite bowls or cups, and eat immediately.

Nutrition Information per serving: 50 Calories, 7 g total fat, 0 mg cholesterol, 5 mg sodium, **12g carbonates (sugars),** 2g fiber, and 1g protein.

ORANGE MUFFINS

Makes:
12 Servings

Preparation time:
30 minutes

Ingredients:
2 cups quinoa flour
1 cup pure stevia
1 tsp. baking powder
1 pinch salt
1 cup orange juice (no sugar added)
1 Tbsp. lemon juice
4 Tbsp. coconut oil
1 large egg
1 tsp. orange zest
1 tsp. lemon zest

Directions:

1. Preheat oven to 350 degrees F.

2. Spray your muffin tins with non-stick cooking spray. Set aside.

3. In a large bowl, mix all dry ingredients: flour, salt, stevia and baking powder.

4. In a different bowl, mix the wet ingredients: orange juice, lemon juice, coconut oil, egg, orange and lemon zests.

5. Combine both mixtures and mix well but don't overdo it.

6. Pour the muffin batter evenly into each muffin tin. Bake for about 20 to 25 minutes.

Nutrition Information per serving: 175 Calories, 7 g total fat, 143 mg cholesterol, 18 mg sodium, **26 g carbonates (sugars),**2g fiber, and 5g protein.

BAKED APPLES

Makes:
8 Servings

Preparation time:
45 minutes

Ingredients:
6-8 apples (depends on how many people you are serving)
1-2 cups water
1 Tbsp. cinnamon
2 Tbsp. orange juice
¼ cup coconut palm sugar
¼ cup coconut flour
2 Tbsp. Manuka honey

Directions:

1. Do not peel the apples. Remove the cores from the top, and also the insides of the apples, leaving the bottom to hold up the filling.

2. Dice the insides of the apples Add the orange juice to the apples, along with the honey.

3. Place back the apple mixture into each apple "shells."

4. In a small bowl, mix the coconut palm sugar and coconut flour. You will then use it as a topping for the apples.

5. Place all apples in a baking dish with the water in the bottom. Bake for about 30 minutes or until the apples are fully cooked.

Nutrition Information per serving: 100 Calories, 0.5 g total fat, 0 mg cholesterol, 5mg sodium, **21 g carbonates (sugars),** 4g fiber, and 0g protein.

TOO GOOD TO BE TRUE CANDIES

Makes:
16 Servings

Preparation time:
35 minutes

Ingredients:
3/4 cup pure stevia
1 cup coconut palm sugar
1/3 cup coconut cream
1/3 cup skim milk
2 Tbsp. gee butter
1 tsp. almond extract
1/2 cup chopped pecans and walnut mix

Directions:

1. Prepare a square baking dish by greasing it. I usually use a little coconut oil.

2. In a large saucepan, combine the coconut palm sugar, stevia, coconut cream and skim milk. Bring the liquid to a boil and then lower the temperature. Let it simmer for about 20 minutes.

3. Add the butter and almond extract and stir only once. Let it cool down.

4. Add the nuts and stir the mix a few times.

5. Pour the mixture into the greased dish and set it aside. When the candy is completely cooled, cut into squares. If needed, refrigerate the candy for a little.

Nutrition Information per serving: 152 Calories, 1.5 g total fat, 6 mg cholesterol, 25 mg sodium, **23 g carbonates (sugars),** 0g fiber, and 1g protein.

THE PERFECT HOLIDAY LOAF

Makes:
12-16 Servings

Preparation time:
45 minutes to 1 hour

Ingredients:
1/3 cup fat-free sour cream
2 cups unsweetened pumpkin puree
3 eggs
2 cups quinoa flour
½ cup almond flour
¼ cup walnut oil
¾ cup pure stevia
2 Tbsp. baking powder
1 Tbsp. Pumpkin pie spice
1 cup dried raisins

Directions:

1. Preheat oven to 350 degrees F.

2. In a large bowl, mix the sour cream, pumpkin puree, eggs and walnut oil.

3. Add the dry ingredients: quinoa flour, almond flour, stevia, baking powder, and spices. Mix well.

4. Add the dried raisins. Mix again and pour this wonderful mixture into a greased loaf pan.

5. Bake for 45-50 minutes. Serve warm or cold.

Nutrition Information per serving: 180 Calories, 6 g total fat, 40 mg cholesterol, 140 mg sodium, **28.5 g carbonates (sugars),** 1.1g fiber, and 5g protein.

PEAR AND HONEY SCONES

Makes:
10 Servings

Preparation time:
15 minutes

Ingredients:
2 cups coconut flour
1 pinch salt
1 Tbsp. baking powder
½ tsp. baking soda
¼ cup flaxseeds
1/3 cup coconut oil
2 chopped finely fresh and ripe pears (peeled)
½ cup skim milk
¼ cup Manuka honey
1 tsp. ground cinnamon

Directions:

1. Preheat oven to 400 degrees F.

2. Combine the dry ingredients in a large mixing bowl: coconut flour, flaxseeds, baking powder, salt and baking soda.

3. Add the coconut oil (room temperature) gradually, while mixing, and then the pears, milk, and honey. Mix until the combination becomes moist.

4. You will be left with a nice dough that can be rolled into a large circle or square.

5. To prepare the scone shape, cut the dough into 10 wedges and bake them on a greased baking sheet for 20 minutes.

Nutrition Information per serving: 223 Calories, 3.8 g total fat, 0 mg cholesterol, 270 mg sodium, **36 g carbonates (sugars),** 2.1g fiber, and 5g protein.

BROWNIES

Makes:
16 Servings

Preparation time:
15 minutes

Ingredients:
1/3 cup coconut oil
1/2 cup unsweetened applesauce
1/2 cup unsweetened cocoa powder
1/2 cup coconut palm sugar
1 cup quinoa flour
1 tsp. baking powder
1/2 tsp. baking soda
2 large eggs
1 tsp. vanilla extract
1/4 cup chopped pecans

Directions:

1. Preheat oven to 375 degrees F.

2. Combine the coconut oil, applesauce and cocoa powder. Add the coconut palm sugar and let it dissolve.

3. Also, add the eggs and vanilla, and mix well.

4. In a separate bowl, combine together the dry ingredients (quinoa flour, baking soda, baking powder). Add this to the first mixture. Mix again.

5. Pour this new batter into the previously greased square baking dish. Sprinkle on the chopped pecans.

6. Bake the brownies for 25 minutes.

7. Cut in squares. Enjoy!

Nutrition Information per serving: 165 Calories, 7 g total fat, 101 mg cholesterol, 85 mg sodium, **21 g carbonates (sugars),** 0.2g fiber, and 3g protein.

SWEET POTATO PIE

Makes:
8 Servings

Preparation time:
15 minutes

Ingredients:
Diabetic friendly pre-cooked pie crust (look for gluten free and the type of flours that you are allowed to eat for your particular diet—no sugar added, of course)
2 cups mashed sweet potatoes (equivalent to 22 or 3 cooked potatoes)
2 medium size eggs
1 cup coconut palm sugar
2 Tbsp. coconut flour
1 Tbsp. Lemon juice
1 tsp. almond extract
½ tsp. ground cloves
½ tsp. cinnamon
1 can coconut milk
Sugar-free whipped cream (optional topping)

Directions:

1. Place the cooked sweet potatoes in a large mixing bowl. Add the coconut palm sugar and lemon juice. Blend the mix in your electric mixer until it is smooth.

2. Add the eggs, almond extract, spices, coconut milk and coconut flour.

3. Pour this sweet potato mixture into the pie crust and cook it for about 40 minutes.

4. Serve the pie warm and with whipped cream. Some people prefer to eat it cold or room temperature, as I do.

Nutrition Information per serving: 197 Calories,67 g total fat, 58 mg cholesterol, 316 mg sodium, **27.5 g carbonates (sugars),** 0.2g fiber, and 7g protein.

HEALTHY DONUTS

Makes:
12 Servings

Preparation time:
20 minutes

Ingredients:
1 1/4 cups almond or coconut flour (your preference)
1/2 tsp. baking soda
1 pinch salt
1/2 cup low fat sour cream
1 egg
1/2 cup pure stevia
2 Tbsp. coconut oil
1 tsp. vanilla
½ tsp. cinnamon
For optional topping: coconut palm sugar

Directions:

1. Preheat oven to 3 degrees F. As you can tell, we are not going to try the donuts, but bake them.

2. You should have a donut pan and spray it with some non-stick baking oil (like coconut oil).

3. In a bowl, combine the chosen flour, baking soda, and salt.

4. In a different bowl, mix the sour cream, stevia, egg, coconut oil and vanilla.

5. Add the wet mixture to the dry one and mix it all together until it is blended.

6. Place batter into the doughnut pan. Do not exceed the mold as it will get messy.

7. Sprinkle the batter with the coconut palm sugar.

8. Bake for about 10 minutes. Watch it closely.

Nutrition Information per serving: 172 Calories, 4 g total fat, 1 mg cholesterol, 180 mg sodium, **32 g carbonates (sugars),** 2g fiber, and 4g protein.

DIABETIC APPROVED PUMPKIN PIE

Makes:

8 Servings

Preparation time:

1-hour

Ingredients:

1 diabetic-friendly pie crust

1 large unsweetened pumpkin puree

2 egg whites

1 cup almond milk

1 pinch salt

½ tsp. ginger

½ tsp. cinnamon

½ tsp. nutmeg

2 Tbsp. sugarcane juice

2 Tbsp. coconut palm sugar

Directions:

1. Preheat oven to 375 degrees F.

2. In a large bowl, mix all the ingredients; they will become your pie filling. Taste and adjust the seasonings if you like.

3. Pour the filling into the pie crust.

4. Bake the food in the oven for 50 minutes and serve it with a scoop of sugar-free whipped cream if you want to.

Nutrition Information per serving: 256 Calories, 3 g total fat, 104 mg cholesterol, 45 mg sodium, **21 g carbonates (sugars),** 0.2g fiber, and 4g protein.

DATE BREAD

Makes:

12 Servings

Preparation time:

45 minutes

Ingredients:

1/2 cup diced dried dates
½ cup cold water
1 cup almond flour
½ cup quinoa flour
1 tsp. baking powder
1 tsp. nutmeg
1 tsp. cinnamon
1 pinch salt
¾ cup coconut palm sugar
½ cup unsweetened almond milk
¼ cup walnut oil
1 large egg
1 tsp. almond extract

Directions:

1. Preheat the oven to 350 degrees F.

2. Prepare a loaf dish by spraying nonstick oil evenly. Set aside.

3. You should place the dates in water, in a small saucepan, and cook them over medium heat for 10-15 minutes, so they get softer. Once done, set them aside to cool down.

4. In a medium size bowl, mix the almond and quinoa flour, salt, baking powder and spices.

5. In a different bowl, combine the other ingredients, except the dates. Then combine both mixtures together to get your loaf batter.

6. Add the dates and mix lightly again. Pour the final batter into the baking dish and bake it in the oven for about 40 minutes.

Nutrition Information per serving: 142 Calories, 5 g total fat, 14 mg cholesterol, 71 mg sodium, **24 g carbonates (sugars),**3g fiber, and 2g protein.

ZUCHINNI CITRUS BREAD

Makes:
10-16 Servings

Preparation time:
1 hour to 1 .5 hour

Ingredients:
1 cup shredded zucchini (peeled)
1 cup almond flour
½ cup coconut flour
½ coconut palm sugar
1 Tbsp. sugarcane juice
1 pinch salt
1/3 cup chopped pistachios
1/3 cup coconut oil
1 Tbsp. lime juice
1 tsp. lime zest
½ cup almond milk
2 large eggs
1 tsp. ginger

Directions:

1. Preheat the oven to 350 degrees F.

2. Grease a loaf pan with coconut oil and set it aside.

3. In a large mixing bowl, combine the flours, coconut palm sugar, baking soda and stir in the shredded zucchini, pistachios, lime zest, lime juice and ginger.

4. Whisk the eggs, almond milk and coconut oil in a separate bowl and add this mixture to the dry one. Mix again.

5. Pour the batter into the baking dish and bake it for about 55 minutes.

Nutrition Information per serving: 122 Calories, 6 g total fat, 24 mg cholesterol, 206 mg sodium, **15 g carbonates (sugars),**1g fiber, and 2g protein.

MUFFINS FILLED WITH PEACHES

Makes:
8-12 Servings

Preparation time:
45 minutes

Ingredients:
1 cup quinoa flour
¼ cup pure stevia
2 tsp. baking powder
1 pinch salt
1 large egg
2 Tbsp. gee butter
2 Tbsp. skim milk
½ cup Peaches sugar-free preserve-jam
¼ tsp. vanilla extract

Directions:

1. Preheat oven to 350 degrees F.

2. Coat the muffin tins with nonstick cooking oil.

3. In a mixing bowl, combine the flour, the stevia, baking powder, and salt.

4. In a separate bowl, whisk the egg, butter, and milk. Combine both mixtures. Add the almond extract after, and mix again.

5. Pour the batter into the muffin tins and bake it for about 22-25 minutes.

Nutrition Information per serving: 150 Calories, 17 g total fat, 35 mg cholesterol, 190 mg sodium, **24 g carbonates (sugars),**0g fiber, and 3g protein.

PEANUT BUTTER DELIGHT

Makes:
8 Servings

Preparation time:
15 minutes

Ingredients:
1/2 cup sugar-free peanut butter
3 Tbsp. coconut palm sugar
2 cups coconut milk
2 egg whites
1 tsp. sugarcane juice
1 Tbsp. orange juice
½ tsp. Orange zest

Directions:

1. You can use the blender or an electric mixer for this one. I prefer the electric mixer; it's just easier to clean!

2. Pour the ingredients into a large bowl and mix them well.

3. Cover your bowl and refrigerate the pudding for a few hours before you serve it.

Nutrition Information per serving: 217 Calories, 9 g total fat, 91 mg cholesterol, 262 mg sodium, **22 g carbonates (sugars),**2g fiber, and 11g protein.

SCOTTISH SCONES

Makes:
16 Servings

Preparation time:
15 minutes

Ingredients:
1 cup quinoa flour
1 cup almond flour
1 tsp. baking powder
1/2 tsp. salt
1 cup fat-free sour cream
2 Tbsp. gee butter
½ cup dried raisins
¼ cup dried cherries

Directions:

1. Preheat your oven to 375 degrees F.
2. Prepare a baking sheet by spraying one with cooking oil.
3. In a mixing bowl, combine the almond flour, baking powder, salt and quinoa flour.
4. Add the butter, sour cream, and mix with your fingers or a fork.
5. Add the dried fruit. Roll the dough until it becomes about ½ inch thick.
6. Cut the dough into 12-16 pieces to form the scones.
7. Bake the dough on the baking sheet for about 20 minutes.

Nutrition Information per serving: 97 Calories, 3 g total fat, 7 mg cholesterol, 115 mg sodium, **16 g carbonates (sugars),**1.5g fiber, and 3g protein.

FRUIT SKEWERS

Makes:
4 Servings

Preparation time:
15 minutes

Ingredients:
2 oranges peeled and in segments
2 apples (large cubed)
1 banana (thickly sliced)
2 Tbsp. unsweetened cocoa powder
3 Tbsp. coconut cream
2 Tbsp. coconut palm sugar

Directions:

1. In a small saucepan, mix the coconut milk, coconut palm sugar and cocoa powder. Bring the liquid to boil (if needed) to get it thick enough so it can be your chocolate sauce.

2. Arrange all fruit as described.

3. Use wooden skewers and one by one poke through each piece of fruit. Assemble the fruit as you wish.

4. Drizzle the chocolate sauce you created onto each skewer.

Nutrition Information per serving: 100 Calories, 1 g total fat, 15 mg cholesterol, 19 mg sodium, **18 g carbonates (sugars),** 1g fiber, and 2g protein.

ORANGE APPLE CLAFOUTI

Makes:
8 Servings

Preparation time:
45 minutes

Ingredients:
2-cups of sugar-free tangerine or clementine slices with juice (from a can is fine)
1 large diced apple (Gala is great)
2 large eggs
4 egg whites
1/3 cup coconut palm sugar
¾ cups unsweetened coconut milk
1 tsp. vanilla
2 Tbsp. no sugar added orange juice (the juice from the can is fine)
1 Tbsp. orange zest
2/3 cup coconut flour
1 pinch salt

Directions:

1. Preheat oven to 375 degrees F.

2. Using the electric mixer, mix the eggs, egg whites, and coconut sugar. Next add the coconut milk, orange juice, and vanilla.

3. Add the orange zest, coconut flour and combine it all together.

4. Use a large baking dish and grease it lightly with coconut oil. Place the fruits in the bottom of the dish and pour the batter on top of it.

5. Bake it in the oven for 30 minutes.

Nutrition Information per serving: 150 Calories, 2 g total fat, 55 mg cholesterol, 100 mg sodium, **25 g carbonates (sugars),** 1g fiber, and 5g protein.

ANGEL FOOD CAKE

Makes:
10-12 Servings

Preparation time:
50 minutes

Ingredients:
1 cup pure stevia or any equivalent
½ cup non-salted ghee butter
2 large eggs
1 ½ cup coconut flour
1 tsp. baking powder
½ cup unsweetened coconut milk
1 Tbsp. orange zest
Topping
4 Tbsp. orange juice (no sugar added)
1 Tbsp. Sugarcane juice
3 Tbsp. coconut palm sugar

Directions:

1. Preheat oven to 350 degrees F.

2. In a large bowl, whisk well the stevia, butter, and eggs. Add all the other ingredients (except the ones for the topping), and combine well.

3. Pour the batter into a greased cake-baking dish. Bake it for about 50 minutes.

4. Meanwhile, prepare the topping by mixing the 3 ingredients in a small saucepan. Add the topping to the cake as soon as it comes out of the oven.

5. Let it cool down for 10 minutes before you start slicing and serving it.

Nutrition Information per serving: 157 Calories, 1 g total fat, 20 mg cholesterol, 230 mg sodium, **15 g carbonates (sugars),** 7g fiber, and 4g protein.

CUTE ELEPHANT EARS

Makes:
24 Servings

Preparation time:
35 minutes

Ingredients:
1 package (1/4 ounce) active dry yeast
1/4 cup warm water
2 cups almond flour
2 Tbsp. pure stevia
1 pinch salt
1/3 cup room temperature coconut oil
1/3 cup unsweetened almond milk
1 large egg
Filling
2 Tbsp. coconut oil
1/2 cup coconut palm sugar
1 Tbsp. cinnamon

Directions:

1. Preheat oven to 375 degrees F.

2. In a bowl, mix the dry yeast with warm water and stir until the yeast is completely dissolved.

3. In a different bowl, mix the almond flour, stevia, and salt. Gradually add the coconut oil and you will obtain a crumbly batter.

4. Add the almond milk and egg. Use your hands to mix the batter and transform it into the dough. Cover the bowl with the dough and put it in the refrigerator for 2 hours.

5. Roll the dough into a large rectangle on a floury surface.

6. Prepare the filling by mixing all the ingredients in a bowl. Sprinkle the filling on the dough and roll the dough as you would for a log. Cut the dough into ½ inch slices.

7. Place the slices on a greased baking sheet and cook them for 9-10 minutes. You should obtain about 24 elephant ears in total.

Nutrition Information per serving: 109 Calories, 14g total fat, 18 mg cholesterol, 76 mg sodium, **18 g carbonates (sugars),** 0g fiber, and 1g protein.

EGGNOG

Makes:
4 Servings

Preparation time:
20 minutes

Ingredients:
1 Tbsp. unflavored gelatin
2 cups reduced-fat and sugar-free eggnog
2 Tbsp. pure stevia
¼ tsp. nutmeg
1/2 tsp. almond extract
1 cup sugar-free whipped topping, divided

Directions:

1. In a medium saucepan, mix the eggnog and gelatin and let it stand for 5 minutes. Start heating the mix on low temperature and gradually stir in the stevia, nutmeg.

2. When all is dissolved, transfer the almond extract into a bowl. Refrigerate it until it's ready to serve. The eggnog will thicken over the next hour and that's exactly what you want.

3. Serve the eggnog with a generous portion of whipped cream.

4. You should be able to serve 4 people with this recipe.

Nutrition Information per serving: 165 Calories, 6g total fat, 97 mg cholesterol, 80 mg sodium, **21 g carbonates (sugars),** 1g fiber, and 7g protein.

STRAWBERRY PARFAIT

Makes:
2-4 Servings

Preparation time:
30 minutes

Ingredients:
1 small sugar-free pack strawberry gelatin (Jello)
1 cup boiling water
2 egg whites
1 cup fresh sliced strawberry
½ cup fresh blueberries
1 Tbsp. chia seeds
1 Tbsp. orange zest

Directions:

1. Dissolve the strawberry gelatin in boiling water and then allow it to cool as instructed on the package. Add the egg whites.

2. Use an electric mixer and mix the *jello* with the egg whites for 6 or 7 minutes.

3. Add the strawberries, blueberries, orange zest and chia seeds. Mix again.

4. Pour the final mixture into fancy cups.

Nutrition Information per serving: 61 Calories, 14g total fat, 0 mg cholesterol, 56 mg sodium, **13 g carbonates (sugars),** 1g fiber, and 3g protein.

DELICIOUS BANANA AND MORE COOKIES

Makes:
30 Servings

Preparation time:
30 minutes

Ingredients:
1.5 cups quinoa flour
½ cup flaxseeds
1 tsp. baking powder
½ tsp. baking soda
1 tsp. cinnamon
1 tsp. vanilla
1 pinch salt
2 large ripe bananas
2 Tbsp. coconut oil
¾ cup coconut palm sugar
3 /4 cup chopped walnuts
2 Tbsp. Manuka honey

Directions:

1. Preheat oven to 350 degrees F.
2. Place nonstick cooking spray on 2 large baking sheets.
3. In a mixing bowl, mash the bananas; add the eggs, vanilla, coconut oil and honey.

4. In a larger bowl, mix the dry ingredients: quinoa flour, flaxseeds, coconut palm sugar, baking soda, baking powder, cinnamon, and salt.

5. Combine the wet mixture into the dry one and mix well.

6. Add the walnuts and mix again. Drop one teaspoon of cookie dough at a time on the baking sheets. You should be able to make 24-30 servings.

7. Bake for 15 minutes or so. Watch closely.

Nutrition Information per serving: 80 Calories, 3g total fat, 5 mg cholesterol, 35 mg sodium, **11.5 g carbonates (sugars),** 1.5g fiber, and 2g protein.

GREEN TEA SMOOTHIE

Makes:
1 serving

Preparation time:
10 minutes

Ingredients:
2 Tbsp. sugar-free green tea powder
3 Tbsp. hot water
1 banana
1 cup almond milk
½ cup ice cubed
1 Tbsp. Manuka honey

Directions:

1. In a bowl, mix the green tea and water together.
2. Blend all the ingredients in your high-speed blender, including the green tea paste.
3. Add more ice cubes if you wish.

Nutrition Information per serving: 95 Calories, 1g total fat, 0 mg cholesterol, 35 mg sodium, **16.5 g carbonates (sugars),** 1.5g fiber, and 2g protein.

BALLS OF GOODNESS

Makes:
24-30 servings

Preparation time:
1.5 hour

Ingredients:
1/3 cup Manuka honey
2 Tbsp. orange juice (no sugar added)
½ cup almond butter
¼ cup flaxseeds
½ cup coconut flour
1/3 dried cranberries
¼ cup chopped cashews
1/4 cup unsweetened flaked coconut
1 Tbsp. sesame seeds

Directions:

1. In a small saucepan, mix in the orange juice and honey, and heat it on low temperature. Remove from heat after 10 minutes.

2. Add the almond butter with the honey mixture, and mix until it becomes smooth.

3. In a large mixing bowl, combine the flaxseeds, coconut flour, cashews, cranberries, coconut flakes and sesame seeds.

4. Pour the honey and almond butter on top of the dry ingredients. Cover the bowl and refrigerate for about 1 hour.

5. When you take the mixture out, it should be ready to mold into balls. You should be able to form 24-20 balls.

Nutrition Information per serving: 153 Calories, 8g total fat, 100 mg cholesterol, 48 mg sodium, **17 g carbonates (sugars),** 2g fiber, and 4g protein.

YUMMY SANDWICH COOKIES

Makes:
24 servings

Preparation time:
10 minutes

Ingredients:
½ cup coconut flour
1 tsp. baking powder
5 eggs
2/3 cup coconut palm sugar
2 cup toasted pecans
½ cup fat-free cream cheese
2 Tbsp. unsweetened cocoa powder
2 Tbsp. skim milk

Directions:

1. Preheat oven to 350 degrees F.

2. Combine in a large bowl the coconut flour, baking powder. Mix well.

3. In the food processor, mix the eggs, coconut palm sugar and nuts. Blend until the mix is almost smooth. Add this new mixture to the flour one.

4. You now have your cookie dough. Form the cookies and place them on a previously greased baking sheet a few inches apart. Bake them for 10 minutes.

5. When the cookies come out, let them cool down and then mix them together in a small bowl of what will be the filling: cream cheese, milk, and cocoa powder.

6. Fill each cookie with a teaspoon of chocolate mixture (like a sandwich; a cookie on the bottom and one of the top).

Nutrition Information per serving: 92 Calories, 4.5g total fat, 10 mg cholesterol, 109 mg sodium, **10 g carbonates (sugars),** 1g fiber, and 3g protein.

BANANA AND BERRY TREAT

Makes:
12 servings

Preparation time:
25 minutes

Ingredients:
1 package of sugar-free vanilla pudding mix
2 tsp. vanilla extract
2 cups unsweetened coconut milk
1 cup sliced fresh strawberries
1 or 2 sliced bananas
2 Tbsp. pure stevia
3 Tbsp. favorite nuts (I prefer chopped pecans)

Directions:

1. Prepare the pudding according to the directions on the package, using the coconut milk. Place it in the refrigerator for now.

2. In a small bowl, place the fresh strawberries with the stevia and vanilla. Mix well.

3. Remove the pudding from the refrigerator. Make sure it is placed in your serving bowl.

4. Place the sliced bananas and the strawberries around the pudding evenly, so it looks pretty.

5. Sprinkle the nuts on top and serve the treat cold.

Nutrition Information per serving: 196 Calories, 2.5g total fat, 25 mg cholesterol, 109 mg sodium, **22 g carbonates (sugars),** 2g fiber, and 3g protein.

CHOCO-CHEESE NO BAKE PIE

Makes:
8 servings

Preparation time:
35 minutes

Ingredients:
2 fat-free packages cream cheese (room temperature)
1 package sugar-free chocolate pudding mix
1 cup unsweetened almond milk
¼ cup water
1 tsp. almond extract
1 cup sugar-free whipped cream

Pie crust:
Sugar-free chocolate cookie crust

Directions:

1. In a large bowl, combine the cream cheese, almond milk, chocolate pudding mix, and water. Mix well.

2. Combine the almond extract and also the whipped cream, with to the first mixture. Mix again.

3. Evenly spread the pie filling on the pre-cooked crust.

4. You can decorate the pie with nuts, carob chips, or just eat it as is because it is definitely smooth and tasty.

Nutrition Information per serving: 202 Calories, 4.5g total fat, 23 mg cholesterol, 100 mg sodium, **25 g carbonates (sugars),** 1g fiber, and 3g protein.

CHOCOLATE MINT PUDDING

Makes:

4-6 serving

Preparation time:

30 minutes

Ingredients:

1 package of sugar-free chocolate pudding mix
3 tbsp. crushed sugar-free peppermints
2 cups unsweetened cashew milk
½ cup sugar-free whipped cream

Directions:

1. Prepare the pudding according to the package directions, using the cashew milk. Refrigerate it for at least 15 minutes.

2. Use a food processor to crush the mints so they are as small as possible.

3. Remove the pudding from the refrigerator; add the whipped cream and the crushed candies. Place into serving bowls. Enjoy!

Nutrition Information per serving: 143 Calories, 2.5g total fat, 12 mg cholesterol, 100 mg sodium, **15 g carbonates (sugars),** 1.5g fiber, and 2g protein.

AVOCADO AND PEANUT BUTTER SHAKE

Makes:
1 serving

Preparation time:
10 minutes

Ingredients:
½ ripe avocado
2 Tbsp. creamy sugar-free peanut butter
1 tsp. lemon juice
1 cup unsweetened cashew milk
1 cup ice cubes

Directions:

1. Blend all the ingredients in a high-speed blender.

2. If the shake becomes too thick, add more ice cubes to it and mix again.

3. When you are happy with the texture, pour it into your tallest cup.

Nutrition Information per serving: 159 Calories, 2.9g total fat, 98 mg cholesterol, 109 mg sodium, **16 g carbonates (sugars),** 1g fiber, and 3g protein.

SIMPLE PINEAPPLE BARS

Makes:
10-12 servings

Preparation time:
1 hour

Ingredients:
Crust
1 ½ cup coconut flour
¼ cup coconut palm sugar
1 pinch salt
¼ cup coconut oil (room temperature)
Filling
2 large eggs
½ cup fat-free sour cream
1/3 cup coconut flour
1 can sugar-free crushed pineapple (drained)
Topping (drizzle)
2 Tbsp. coconut milk
1/3 cup coconut palm sugar

Directions:

1. Preheat oven to 350 degrees F.

2. To prepare the crust, mix all the ingredients in a bowl. Press the mix into a greased rectangle baking dish and bake the mix in the oven for about 20 minutes

3. In a different bowl, combine the eggs, sour cream, and coconut flour. Gradually add the crushed pineapple, and stir well. Evenly spread this mixture on the cooled down crust.

4. Place the mix in the oven for another 45 to 50 minutes.

5. Meanwhile, mix together the topping ingredients. When the dessert is done, cut it into bars.

Nutrition Information per serving: 159 Calories, 2.9g total fat, 98 mg cholesterol, 109 mg sodium, **16 g carbonates (sugars),** 1g fiber, and 3g protein.

Printed in Great Britain
by Amazon

71836997R00113